Jim,

Let's make

Barry Potter

D1189615

*Published by:*

# TODAY IS YESTERDAY'S TOMORROW™

*— America's Publishing Company*

# PRESIDENTIAL
# LESSONS LEARNED

# FOLLOW
# THE LEADER

*By: Bill Porter, An American Citizen*

**Published by:**

 **TODAY IS YESTERDAY'S TOMORROW**™

*— America's Publishing Company*

*Published by: Today is Yesterday's Tomorrow*
*4320 Suwanee Dam Road, Suite 2600*
*Suwanee, Georgia, 30024*
678.714.6223
www.FollowTheLeaderUSA.com

*Copyright © 2008*
*All rights reserved.*

*ISBN 978-0-9771298-1-0*

*TYT, Today is Yesterday's Tomorrow, and colophon are trademarks of Today is Yesterday's Tomorrow, Inc.*

*Book Layout and Cover Design by Pam Griffing.*

*Written, published, printed and distributed in the United States of America.*

*10 9 8 7 6 5 4 3 2 1*

*Cover pictures courtesy of:*
*Lyndon Baines Johnson Library & Museum, Jimmy Carter Library & Museum, William J. Clinton Presidential Library & Museum and John F. Kennedy Presidential Library & Museum.*

---

**ATTENTION CORPORATIONS, ASSOCIATIONS, COLLEGES, AND ORGANIZATIONS:** Quantity discounts are available on bulk purchases of this book for educational purposes or fund raising. Special books or book excerpts can also be created to fit specific needs.

For information, please contact TYT Sales Department:
678.714.6223
www.FollowTheLeaderUSA.com

---

*Dedicated to*

MOMMERS AND POPPERS
JAN, BILLY, CINDI, ALEXIS AND JACK

# CONTENTS

SPECIAL RECOGNITION                                                      IX
ACKNOWLEDGEMENTS                                                         X
PREFACE                                                                  XIII

CHAPTER ONE        CAMPAIGN PROMISES THAT END UP          1
                   AS FAILED LEGISLATION
                   ARE MISSED OPPORTUNITIES!

                   PRESIDENTIAL TIME LINE &              23
                   CONGRESSIONAL MAJORITIES

CHAPTER TWO        PRESIDENT JOHN F. KENNEDY             35
                   THE APOLLO SPACE PROGRAM
                   AN OPPORTUNITY SEIZED!

CHAPTER THREE      PRESIDENT LYNDON B. JOHNSON           61
                   THE GREAT SOCIETY PROGRAM
                   ANOTHER OPPORTUNITY SEIZED!

CHAPTER FOUR       PRESIDENT JIMMY CARTER                95
                   AMERICA'S COMPREHENSIVE
                   NATIONAL ENERGY PLAN
                   A MISSED OPPORTUNITY!

CHAPTER FIVE       PRESIDENT BILL CLINTON                137
                   AMERICA'S COMPREHENSIVE
                   NATIONAL HEALTHCARE PLAN
                   ANOTHER MISSED OPPORTUNITY!

CHAPTER SIX        AUTHOR'S REFLECTIONS                  165
                   & LESSONS LEARNED

CHAPTER SEVEN      A NEW IDEA FOR AMERICA                185

THOUGHTS ABOUT CHANGE                                                   195
BOOK SERIES DESCRIPTION & PREVIEWS                                      197
NOTES                                                                   203

# SPECIAL RECOGNITION

*Bill Porter, Sr.* made an incredible contribution to the evolution of this book by tirelessly providing a critical and circumspect analysis of the content, word choice and grammar. His continual review and critiquing significantly increased the quality and readability of each of the chapters. I not only appreciate his input and involvement because of the professionalism that he added, but I also enjoyed the interaction of working collaboratively with my father. It will always be one of my most cherished memories.

*Thank You Poppers!*

*Cindi Porter* provided not only all of the preliminary editing, but she was also instrumental with the creative design and layout of both the book and the cover. She is my primary intellectual sounding board and my ideas consultant. Working closely with my daughter on a day to day basis has been truly one of life's blessings.

*Thank You Cindi!*

*Ray Anderson* is an extraordinary American citizen who really cares deeply about our country. His feedback and unique opinions were instrumental in helping to clarify many of the issues and also to reach many of the eventual conclusions. His energy and genuine interest in America's future provided not only assistance but also inspiration.

*Thank You Ray!*

*Dr. Margaret Gorman* is an exceptional professor at The George Washington University. She helped design the conceptual framework for this study. Her encouragement and moral support were both vital and much appreciated.

*Thank You Margaret!*

---

*Coming together is a beginning;*
*Keeping together is progress;*
*Working together is success.*

— HENRY FORD

---

*"The quality of a person's life is in direct proportion of their commitment to excellence, regardless of their chosen field of endeavor."*

— Vincent T. Lombardi

# ACKNOWLEDGEMENTS

The majority of the information in this book was based on the outstanding research from the dissertations and the supporting documents of the following scholars. Their contribution to the body of knowledge that has been accumulated about the issues and events that are discussed is a national asset. Furthermore, the level of excellence that each of these brilliant scholars demonstrated in their work was a source of inspiration for me and a reminder of America's need to always pursue excellence. For as we all know, "Good Enough" usually never is! I thank each of these Americans for a job well done!

*Thought is the seed of action.*
— Ralph Waldo Emerson

*The U.S. Space Program: A Case Study of*
*Non-incremental Policy*
Louis Frank Giacchino — 1983
Georgetown University

*The Apollo Decision and its Lessons for Policy-Makers*
John M. Logsdon — 1970
The George Washington University

*Lawrence F. O'Brien, the Democratic Party and the Nation*
Richard Scott Harris — 1998
The University of Texas at Austin

*Building Presidential Coalitions in Congress:*
*Legislative Liaison in the Johnson White House*
Eric Lyle Davis — 1977
Stanford University

*President Johnson and the 89th Congress:*
*A Functional Analysis of a System under Stress*
Philip West Borst — 1969
Claremont Graduate School and University Center

*An Era of Limits: Jimmy Carter and the*
*Quest for a National Energy Policy*
John Costley Barrow III — 1996
Vanderbilt University

*Fitting an Elephant through a Keyhole:*
*America's Struggle with National Health Insurance*
*in the Twentieth Century*
Kimberly Green Weathers — 2004
University of Houston

■ ■ ■

*"We are continually faced by great opportunities
brilliantly disguised as insoluble problems."*

— UNKNOWN

> *"If you do not change your direction*
> *— you will end up where you are headed."*
>
> — CHINESE PROVERB

# PREFACE

Sooner or later, every major society in recorded history has either collapsed, been defeated or mysteriously disappeared. Are modern American presidents leading our country in a way that will enhance our prospects or endanger our future?

As citizens of the United States, every four years we have the opportunity to vote for the person that will guide our country for the next four to eight years. If capable, this person's strong leadership ability will set us on a course that will hopefully turn campaign rhetoric into legislative reality.

With bold visions of new frontiers, this person will lead our country to new heights, offer solutions to cure the ills of our society and ingenious new ways to pay for it all. Well, maybe — or maybe not! First, he or she will have to get his or her agenda past armies of special interest groups and secondly, he or she will have to eventually win over a majority of the Congress.

Those two formidable obstacles have stopped some of the most well intentioned and charismatic presidents dead in their tracks. Though he meant well, Jimmy Carter's incredible ineptness at dealing with both of those obstacles resulted in a futile attempt to pass a comprehensive national energy program.

This failure dealt a devastating blow to our national security, our economy, and our national confidence. At that time in 1979, a gallon of gas cost only 78 cents.[1] Today with gas at over $4.00 a gallon, we are paying dearly for having missed the opportunity to address our energy problems nearly thirty years ago.

TODAY WITH GAS AT OVER $4.00 A GALLON, WE ARE PAYING DEARLY FOR HAVING MISSED THE OPPORTUNITY TO ADDRESS OUR ENERGY PROBLEMS NEARLY THIRTY YEARS AGO.

For most Americans, there is a sinking feeling that the hour is getting very late. Looking for some way to make a contribution, I have spent the last three years working toward a doctorate degree at The George Washington University in the executive leadership program. The resulting research yielded not only fascinating true stories of contemporary attempts at presidential leadership (both successful and unsuccessful), but perhaps also a tremendous learning tool for future presidents.

As Americans, we really care about our future as well as the future of our children and grandchildren. Let us examine which strategies worked and which ones did not work for four former presidents. With that information, we can make a more educated decision as to which candidate might be our most effective president.

When the endless political advertisements, debates, bumper stickers, blogs, television commercials, and campaign promises are behind us in November, we will have chosen a president to lead our country forward and to address a long laundry list of national issues, problems, and opportunities.

National security, the economy, education, the environment, immigration, taxes, funding (for Social Security, Medicare and Medicaid), infrastructure, jobs, healthcare, the deficits (trade and budget), crime, the absence of a coherent post-Cold War foreign policy, congressional term limits, management of our water resources, our dependency on foreign energy sources, our lack of a wealth creation index, and many other critical issues all require immediate attention and demand workable solutions.

Those solutions will require the support of a majority of the American people and a majority of the Congress. Regardless of all of the campaign rhetoric, if the new president cannot forge a consensus on specific proposed solutions, we will not have chosen a capable leader.

As voters, we must raise the bar for presidential competence. In general, the media has been incredibly ineffective at forcing the candidates to reveal if they actually have a concrete plan for each of these issues and, if they do, to explain their plans in specific detail. The last chapter of this book will offer a plan to assist the media in this regard. If utilized, it will significantly change the format and structure of presidential campaigns in the future as well as the role of the media during the final months leading up to a presidential election.

This plan can significantly improve the performance of both the media and the candidates while giving "real" information to the deciding voters. "We the People" are still in control of our government and our institutions; we have both the opportunity and the responsibility to inject our input into the affairs of our country.

Let's begin!

■  ■  ■

*... that government of the people, **by the people**, for the people, shall not perish from the earth.*

— LINCOLN, GETTYSBURG ADDRESS

# CAMPAIGN PROMISES THAT END UP AS FAILED LEGISLATION

# ARE MISSED OPPORTUNITIES!

*I like things to happen; and if they don't happen,*
*I like to make them happen.*

— WINSTON CHURCHILL

## PRESIDENTS MUST BE LEADERS!

At this point in world history, the president of the United States is widely regarded as the most influential person on the planet. While some may dispute this premise and others may dislike it, the fact remains that in the foreseeable future actions of U.S. presidents will affect not only the lives of millions of people around the world but also in an environmental context, perhaps the life of the planet itself.

Thus, the leadership role of the President of the United States today may be more important than at any other time in world history. Yet the complexity of today's issues requires that future presidents must possess a broader and more diverse set of leadership skills than their predecessors.

A Pulitzer Prize winner, presidential historian, and recognized expert on leadership, James MacGregor Burns introduced the concept of transformational leadership (inspiring and motivational) in 1978 and differentiated it from the simple everyday transactional leadership of "If you'll vote for my proposal, I'll do something else for you."[1]

Burns often refers to Franklin D. Roosevelt as the

quintessential example of an inspirational president who stirred and captured the imagination of the majority of Americans with his visions and dreams and was thus able to gain passage of a legislative agenda that significantly transformed the political landscape of America. Mahatma Gandhi, John Kennedy, Martin Luther King, Jr., and Ronald Reagan are examples of other leaders who also changed the course of history by the power of their transformational leadership.

Burns characterized this kind of leadership as a higher level dynamic than the basic give and take of everyday transactional leadership. Some leaders' vision and imagination can draw others in as followers and participants. However, he goes on to point out that an appropriate blend of this special ability as well as everyday horse trading is usually essential in order to accomplish the grand visions of a president or any other significant leader.

For example, Burns cites Franklin D. Roosevelt as a president whose broad and far-reaching vision of the New Deal came to fruition only as a result of Roosevelt's adroit and intuitive utilization of both transactional and transformational leadership skills. In 2003, Burns reported the following:

> *I found transactional leadership an inadequate tool of analysis for the broader and deeper dimensions of his (Roosevelt's) actions. He had become what his example inspired me to call a transforming leader, just as Lincoln*

*had midway through the Civil War. He had been both a lion and a fox, but now the lion prevailed.*[2]

Conversely, in 2006, Burns contrasted presidents like Roosevelt and Lincoln, who each possessed the full range of leadership capabilities, with other presidents whose leadership lacked the uplifting and motivational component.[3] Burns and his fellow leadership scholar, Georgia Sorenson, describe Bill Clinton's attempt to secure passage of his national healthcare initiative as a prime example of presidential leadership that failed primarily because it lacked this important dimension.[4]

Recently, however, in his new book *Running Alone*, Burns, a self avowed liberal Democrat, refers to this distinct but scarce characteristic of leadership and laments that "We need such vital and creative leadership as we confront the daunting challenges of the twenty-first century, but to get it we must reverse nearly a half century of decline."[5]

For many people including Burns, recent presidential leadership seems to lack the total range of skills that is necessary to adequately lead the United States in an era of increasing volatility and complexity.

Lee Iacocca, the former CEO of Chrysler, recently wrote a new book titled, *"Where Have All the Leaders Gone?"* that captures the mood of many Americans. Scholarly journals such as *American Psychologist* that have not typically reported about leadership research have recently focused much attention on the subject. Presidential leadership is clearly one target of their concern and research. In January 2007 in the *Forward to a Special Issue on Leadership,* Robert J. Sternberg wrote:

> *The United States became a great nation because of the leadership skills of the Founding Fathers. Whether it will remain a great nation will depend, in large part, on the leadership skills of those in power today. Historically, great nations have risen and later fallen in large part as a result of the success or failure of their leadership.*

---

*There is no substitute for the effective use of political skills to advance the cause of a great idea. Ideas are great arrows, but there has to be a bow. And politics is the bow of idealism.*

— BILL MOYERS

---

The widespread uneasiness about presidential leadership appears to reach all corners of American society. David Gergen was a former presidential advisor for Presidents Nixon, Ford, Reagan, and Clinton. He is currently the Director of the Center for Public Leadership at the John F. Kennedy School of Government at Harvard and editor at large at U.S. News & World Report. On June 26, 2006, he wrote:

> *The grim truth is that the political leadership of the country, especially in Washington, is almost dysfunctional in grappling with the big issues bearing down on us. From energy to education, climate change to healthcare, budget deficits to trade deficits, progress is perilously slow. And time is definitely not on our side.*[6]

5

While the nation is still divided on the proper role of the federal government in general terms, the vast majority of Americans agree that there are some things that only the federal government can realistically manage. National defense, our monetary system, international trade issues, interstate transportation, and regulation of the financial service industries are just some examples where few people would debate the necessity of having the federal government handle such affairs.

## TODAY IS YESTERDAY'S TOMORROW

Irrespective of our philosophical differences, most Americans recognize that during the last fifty years the world has changed dramatically. The America that was once divided over whether or not to remain isolated from the rest of the world and "foreign affairs" (i.e. World Wars I + II), no longer has the luxury of that debate.

Future presidential leadership will be required to address both significant domestic and international matters. Whether we like it or not, most would agree that we are members of the world community, and we will have to effectively deal with all of the requirements that accompany that membership.

No issue more clearly focuses that requirement than our continued and increasing dependence on foreign oil and gas. On February 2, 2007, the Wall Street Journal reported that Russia and Iran are attempting to form an organization similar to OPEC for natural gas. India and China have recently emerged as rapidly developing nations, and like Americans and Europeans, their nearly three billion citizens (almost ten times the U.S. population) also want automobiles and other energy related items.

It is obvious that things are not going to just work themselves out. Many more people will be chasing the same dwindling supplies of finite fossil fuels. The obvious conclusion to the current course of events is a world-wide energy dance to the tune of musical chairs — unless we change the tune!

> THE OBVIOUS CONCLUSION TO THE CURRENT COURSE OF EVENTS IS A WORLD-WIDE ENERGY DANCE TO THE TUNE OF MUSICAL CHAIRS — UNLESS WE CHANGE THE TUNE!

A vast majority of Americans, according to poll after poll, agree upon the need for a national approach to our country's energy needs. Yet, despite the fact that gasoline is now approaching $5.00 a gallon and that U.S. troops are stationed and dying in multiple mid-eastern, oil-rich countries, it has been nearly thirty years since Jimmy Carter unsuccessfully attempted to pass a comprehensive national energy policy.

Because of our country's continued reliance on foreign oil supplies, few would argue that we are better off today as a result of that failure, and most would agree that our national security, not to mention our economy, has been seriously compromised.

The likelihood of another attempt by a U.S. president to pass a comprehensive energy policy is quite high. This offers us an excellent example of why we need a better understanding of the organizational and leadership skills that will be required for a future president to successfully secure its enactment. None of the last four presidents, three Republicans (Reagan, Bush I, and Bush II) and one Democrat (Clinton) offered comprehensive legislation that would address this critical issue.

## IT TAKES A PRESIDENT

In January 2008, Hillary Clinton, while campaigning for the democratic nomination for president, caused a furor by proclaiming on Martin Luther King's birthday that "Dr. King's dream began to be realized when President Lyndon Johnson passed the Civil Rights Act of 1964," something that "took a president" to get done.

Despite any real or imagined belittlement of Dr. King and his life's work, her point is beyond debate. Without a president successfully turning a major cause, issue, or idea into an enacted piece of legislation, it remains merely conversation and not yet reality. That will certainly be true of a comprehensive national energy program.

The Civil Rights Act of 1964 that Hillary Clinton was

referring to was one of many successful pieces of *The Great Society* program secured by President Johnson over 40 years ago. There has not been a federal program since then that has expanded the role of the federal government in such a significant way.

The two largest successful presidential initiatives since that time which meet the definition of a non-incremental policy initiative (very large in scope and enacted all at once) did just the opposite. They were the two largest tax cuts in U.S. history.

However, those reductions in the domestic role of the federal government, as opposed to an increased role, have generally defined the direction of contemporary presidential leadership for both Republicans and Democrats for the past few decades. This book will only address four domestic issues within the United States and will not include international initiatives such as the war in Iraq.

Following Lyndon Johnson, who was the most prolific presidential legislator in American history, Presidents Carter and Clinton both became mired in the muck of middling mediocrity in terms of significant legislative accomplishments.

Burns theorizes that neither the Democratic Party nor its two most recent presidents (Carter and Clinton) were unified as a team during the election process. In his recent book *Running Alone*, Burns chides fellow Democrats Jimmy Carter and Bill Clinton for failing to remain loyal to their party during their campaigns. He suggests that they failed to assist other lower level democratic candidates to ride their coattails, and thus they were intentionally **running alone**.[7]

After their victories, Burns contends that Carter and Clinton lacked the requisite democratic support that they needed to pass significant legislation and thus deliver on their campaign promises. He contends that their deliberate "outsider" strategy, successful as a campaign tactic, left them without a solid and loyal congressional base that would cooperate and assist them to pass their agendas. Perhaps, however, there are additional factors that contributed to the success or failure of the four policy initiatives under review.

## WHAT ARE THE QUESTIONS?

The main question that this book will explore is why Presidents Kennedy and Johnson were able to secure passage of major legislation that would have monumental impact on the future of our country while Presidents Carter and Clinton were not. The incredible fact that all four democratic presidents had the extraordinary advantage of having a democratic majority in both the Senate and House of Representatives during the first two years of their presidency is perplexing given their extremely different results.

The contrast of these two successes and two failures conveniently affords us the opportunity to observe what worked well and what did not. The cultural influences of the different time periods, the chemistry of the interaction between the various players, the evolving role of the media, and the ebb and flow of the general mood of the American people were no doubt all contributing factors in each of the four events that will be examined.

However, it is possible and probable that some common factors were present in all four instances and would typically be present in most legislative initiatives. An attempt to identify those factors, as well as how each president dealt with them, will be addressed in the following chapters. The obvious additional questions are:

THE INCREDIBLE FACT THAT ALL FOUR DEMOCRATIC PRESIDENTS HAD THE EXTRAORDINARY ADVANTAGE OF HAVING A DEMOCRATIC MAJORITY IN BOTH THE SENATE AND HOUSE OF REPRESENTATIVES DURING THE FIRST TWO YEARS OF THEIR PRESIDENCY IS PERPLEXING GIVEN THEIR EXTREMELY DIFFERENT RESULTS.

1. What significant common or contrasting factors, if any, were present in all four legislative attempts?

2. What identifiable factors have been reliable predictors of legislative success or failure?

3. What are the lessons that we can learn from these four episodes in recent U.S. history that can help future presidents secure legislative passage of their important campaign promises?

If similarities (whether in success or failure) do surface, and if we can determine that these similarities were significant factors in their respective episodes, then potential patterns of strategy, tactics, personnel choices, timing, publicity, media relations, congressional relationships, and other important factors can be identified and offer future presidents the benefit of lessons learned from these former presidents.

In order to gain the support of millions of Americans as well as a majority of the Congress, any president who will attempt to pursue his or her vision will have to negotiate many hurdles, juggle many competing interests, design an overall strategy, make adjustments along the way, select new tactics, and maintain the necessary balance of numerous contending factors. That is the essence of presidential leadership.

All of these issues would require specific presidential skills. Some would be transformational and motivating in nature. For example, convincing the American people that we need a new cultural attitude about our use of energy and the environment (a certain prerequisite to a comprehensive energy plan) would require extraordinary presidential leadership skills.

In other instances, the back and forth of everyday leadership would be the appropriate tool. For example, supporting a Congress member's pet legislative proposal in return for his or her vote for the energy bill would be a classic, every day event.

However, the ability to skillfully use the full range of leadership capabilities will undoubtedly help determine the degree of legislative success that a president will achieve. If someone has never been president before, then the best preparation for that role would be to study how former presidents have dealt with similar challenges.

Burns and others lament that there has not been a recent democratic president who has possessed the necessary combination of leadership abilities. Many Americans are looking for a president who can pass significant federal legislation that would follow the legislative success of Presidents Roosevelt and Johnson.

Unless that skill set can be identified and discussed publicly during presidential campaigns, it is unlikely that a person possessing or acquiring those qualities will be elected president. Unless the public is aware of the importance of these skills, it is unlikely that politicians will feel the need to master them and demonstrate their proficiency.

Many people have concluded that the complexities of today's political environment are far too great for any one person to navigate. However, others (including this writer) suspect that there may be other factors that also cause or contribute to the success or failure of presidential initiatives.

**THE SKILLS NECESSARY FOR A PROFESSIONAL CAMPAIGNER ARE SIGNIFICANTLY DIFFERENT THAN THE SKILLS THAT WILL BE NECESSARY TO ACTUALLY LEAD A NATION.**

The skills necessary for a professional campaigner are significantly different than the skills that will be necessary to actually lead the nation. Gathering the votes of American citizens in an age of television, internet, and 300 million dollar campaigns is quite different from securing the votes of a majority of Congress once a person has been elected president.

There is not a mentoring program to prepare or train new presidents. The closest approximation would be to have first been the vice president before assuming the responsibilities of the presidency. Of the four presidents under review, only Johnson had that experience, and not surprisingly, he was indisputably the most productive legislator of the group.

Every significant task usually involves a learning curve. Whether it is walking, talking, riding a bicycle, driving a car, or passing a piece of monumental policy legislation, there are distinct benefits from learning lessons from others. How well have recent presidents learned important lessons from their predecessors? Have they learned valuable lessons by studying the mistakes of others, or have they needlessly repeated earlier blunders?

Perhaps it would make sense to develop a legislative blueprint or a "set of instructions of dos and don'ts." A legislative check list, based on the experiences of former presidents, could be a useful tool for future presidents.

While each new president is a unique person and the context of the times is also a differentiating factor, there are some factors that never change such as the need to assemble a majority of the votes in Congress in order to pass a piece of legislation. It requires 218 votes in the House and 51 in the Senate to just eke out passage of a bill. Since potential votes can be "won or lost" depending upon numerous different factors, it is imperative that multiple considerations are simultaneously being addressed by the administration.

It appears, however, that the office of a modern presidency does not draw from a deep well of accumulated memory from former administrations. Since the Democrats and Republicans are constantly trading spots in the White House, perhaps lessons learned are not being passed on to new administrations.

Only Johnson had the benefit of assuming office directly after a fellow Democrat, and he was clearly the most successful at implementing his agenda. This is an important dimension of this study because if new presidents are not benefiting from the learned experiences of former presidents, their learning curve will be much steeper.

Sometimes this concentrated focus of keeping all of the legislative balls in the air must be maintained for many months or even years at a time. Anticipatory planning and strategizing are necessary to determine when to use the basic tactics of barter, reward, and threats or when to employ the potential of inspirational approaches that can appeal to a person or a group's higher sense of propriety and motivation.

Assessing the potential results of both approaches with each of the 535 "voters" is part of the strategic process. Lyndon Johnson wrote the book. Unfortunately, Jimmy Carter and Bill Clinton never read it!

## WHY STUDY ONLY DEMOCRATIC PRESIDENTS?

The first question that nearly every person asked after reading a draft of this book is why only democratic presidents were reviewed. There are three distinct reasons. First, for the last 16 years, the country has been sharply divided along distinct party lines. However, while there has always been a healthy political difference of opinion among the American people, the Clinton/Bush era has produced a venomous political atmosphere that has poisoned the well of public discourse. Hostility and anger have replaced discussion and dialogue.

By limiting the research to just one party, hopefully we can avoid the undermining effect of partisan politics and not instantly lose half of the readers who may think that the party that they love to hate may be receiving favored treatment.

The second reason is because this book does have a focus that would make the democratic presidents the likely choice for review. I believe that most Americans would agree that in general, Republicans feel that less federal government is the best philosophy, and Democrats feel that the federal government is first tool of choice for a long list of societal issues. This book is not addressing that political discussion. It is merely recognizing that some of our country's major problems and opportunities (i.e. immigration, economic policy, and energy, etc.) will be administered at the federal level. Whenever those occasions do arise, the question is *whether or not the president will be able to deliver*. The answer to **that question** is the target of this book.

The third reason is that from 1933 until 1995, the Democratic Party virtually controlled both the House of Representatives and the Senate. While there were six Democrats and six Republicans who served as president during those 62 years, all of them had to work with a legislature that was almost always heavily controlled by the Democrats. Of the 31 congressional two-year sessions that convened during those years, the Democrats controlled the House of Representatives 29 times and the Senate 26 times.

It would be a fair statement to say that, for the most part, the Democrats deserve most of the credit as well as most of the blame for America's fortunes up to that point in our country's modern history. The first three presidents under review presided during that time period. The domestic agendas of all four democratic presidents were a significant extension of the unfinished agenda of Franklin Roosevelt.

A time line at the end of this chapter provides a brief history of the flow of national and world events since FDR was first elected. It also provides the numerical composition of the congressional parties. The dominance of the Democratic Party for 62 years is a critical factor in the modern history of the United States.

However, it is important to note that the Democratic Party underwent a tremendous transformation in the late 1960's and the early 1970's. The proud and noble party that had championed the progressive agendas of Franklin Roosevelt and Lyndon Johnson evolved from progressive to obstructionist. National interests were generally replaced by the agendas of numerous special interest groups. Even democratic presidents (Carter and Clinton) who later offered progressive programs for energy and healthcare would find that the major goal of most democratic congressmen was their own re-election — not the agenda for America.

Eventually, public discontent reached the tipping point. In 1994, for the first time in 40 years, the Republicans replaced the Democrats as the dominant party in both the House and the Senate. That time frame included the last six years of the Clinton administration.

In 2006, the Democrats once again regained control of both the House and the Senate. If that trend continues, the future of the Democratic Party will come to a fork in the road. If the modern Democratic Party reverts back to the progressive policies of FDR and LBJ, its agenda would be extensive and profound. If, however, it resurfaces again as an obstructionist party with only a limited agenda of special interest group proposals, America's future would look considerably different. The answer to that decision may be more important than who is chosen as the next president!

IF THAT TREND CONTINUES, THE FUTURE OF THE DEMOCRATIC PARTY WILL COME TO A FORK IN THE ROAD.

## LIMITATIONS

This study is not meant to generate an opinion of the overall results of any of the individual presidencies or of the presidents themselves. It is only reviewing one legislative attempt of each of the four presidents, and it does not refer to any other issues that they may have addressed or failed to address. It does, however, deal with what is widely recognized as the legislative centerpiece of each of the four administrations.

Furthermore, this research does not take a position on the merits of any of the four individual initiatives. It is strictly limited to analyzing the presidential leadership actions that were present and would typically be present in any major policy initiative. The goal is to aid any future president in his or her attempt to successfully secure congressional approval of a significant piece of legislation.

Chapters two through five will each review the presidential leadership of Presidents Kennedy, Johnson, Carter, and Clinton respectively, in each of their attempts to gain congressional approval of the singular most important legislative attempt of their presidency. Chapter Six will offer a cross case comparison of the four episodes that will reveal the commonalities and differences in the strategic approach of each of the presidents, and thus the lessons that can be learned. The results are startling!

THE RESULTS ARE STARTLING!

The last chapter will offer an idea that could significantly improve the quality and ultimately the results of the presidential campaigns that we experience every four years. The quality of the process can have a definite impact upon the quality of the election results. The idea offered may not be the best one; however, it may start a national conversation that produces a better one. That is a goal worth pursuing.

The following chapters will review, in chronological order, the legislative episodes of the four presidents as well as their successes or failures. While the first story happened nearly 50 years ago, it may offer us the most important lesson that we can utilize today.

■  ■  ■

*It is best to learn from the mistakes of others —*
*We won't have time to make them all ourselves.*

— ANONYMOUS

# PRESIDENTIAL TIME LINE

# &

# CONGRESSIONAL MAJORITIES

# 1933 - 2009

| "A nation that forgets its past can function no better than an individual with amnesia."<br>— David McCullough, Historian | **Franklin Delano Roosevelt**<br>32nd President<br>(1933 - 1945)<br>Democrat |
|---|---|

| | **1933 - 1937** |
|---|---|

**Major Events**

**in the**

**Time Line**

**of the**

**United States**

**and the**

**World**

**1933 - 2009**

- ➢ **THE NEW DEAL PROGRAMS**
- ➢ **BANK HOLIDAY** declared to avert a run on the nation's banks.
- ➢ **CIVILIAN CONSERVATION CORPS (CCC)** - work created for 2,000,000 men (welfare required work - people's dignity maintained).
- ➢ **FEDERAL EMERGENCY RELIEF ACT** - grants to states to provide relief to the American people.
- ➢ **FEDERAL SECURITIES ACT**
- ➢ **NATIONAL RECOVERY ADMIN.**
- ➢ **PUBLIC WORKS ADMINISTRATION**
- ➢ **FEDERAL BANK DEPOSIT INSURANCE CORP. (FDIC)**
- ➢ **NATIONAL LABOR BOARD**
- ➢ **CIVIL WORKS ADMIN.**
- ➢ **SOCIAL SECURITY ACT**
- ➢ **SECURITIES EXCHANGE COMMISSION**
- ➢ **NEUTRALITY ACT** - attempt to avoid U.S. involvement in World Wars.

| HOUSE MAJORITY | | |
|---|---|---|
| House Majority: ➡ | DEM — 313 | DEM — 322 |
| **SENATE MAJORITY** | | |
| Senate Majority: ➡ | DEM — 59 | DEM — 69 |
| **Congressional Representation** | **73rd Congress** | **74th Congress** |
| HOUSE MINORITY | | |
| House Minority: ➡ | REP — 117 | REP — 103 |
| SENATE MINORITY | | |
| Senate Minority: ➡ | REP — 36 | REP — 25 |

# Franklin Delano Roosevelt

## 32nd President
## (1933 - 1945)
## Democrat

| 1937 - 1941 | 1941 - 1945 |
|---|---|
| ➢ NATIONAL HOUSING ACT | ➢ LEND-LEASE ACT - U.S. lends war materials to Britain. |
| ➢ FAIR LABOR STANDARDS ACT - 40 hour work week, increased minimum wage. | ➢ GERMANY INVADES THE SOVIET UNION |
| ➢ FARMS SECURITIES ADMIN. - low interest loans to small farmers. | ➢ GERMAN U-BOAT ATTACKS THE U.S. DESTROYER *KEARNEY* |
| ➢ NAZI GERMANY ANNEXES AUSTRIA | ➢ GERMANY ATTACKS AND SINKS THE U.S. DESTROYER *REUBEN JAMES* |
| ➢ GERMANY INVADES CZECHOSLOVAKIA | ➢ JAPAN ATTACKS UNITED STATES - sneak attack on Pearl Harbor. |
| ➢ ITALY INVADES ALBANIA | ➢ U.S. DECLARES WAR ON JAPAN |
| ➢ GERMANY INVADES POLAND | ➢ GERMANY & ITALY DECLARE WAR ON U.S. |
| ➢ USSR INVADES FINLAND | ➢ MAJOR BATTLES IN THE PACIFIC - CORAL SEA, MIDWAY, GUADALCANAL |
| ➢ GERMANY INVADES NORWAY | |
| ➢ GERMANY INVADES DENMARK | ➢ BATTLE OF THE BULGE |
| ➢ FRANCE & ENGLAND DECLARE WAR ON GERMANY | ➢ INTERNATIONAL ESTABLISHMENT OF THE WORLD BANK & THE INTERNATIONAL MONEY FUND (IMF) |
| ➢ GERMANY ATTACKS BRITAIN | |
| ➢ SELECTIVE TRAINING & SERVICE ACT - first peace-time military draft in U.S. History. | |

| HOUSE MAJORITY | | | |
|---|---|---|---|
| DEM — 334 | DEM — 262 | DEM — 267 | DEM — 222 |

| SENATE MAJORITY | | | |
|---|---|---|---|
| DEM — 76 | DEM — 69 | DEM — 66 | DEM — 57 |

| 75th Congress | 76th Congress | 77th Congress | 78th Congress |
|---|---|---|---|

| HOUSE MINORITY | | | |
|---|---|---|---|
| REP — 88 | REP — 169 | REP — 162 | REP — 209 |

| SENATE MINORITY | | | |
|---|---|---|---|
| REP — 16 | REP — 23 | REP — 28 | REP — 38 |

# Harry S. Truman

### 33rd President
### (1945 - 1953)
### Democrat

| 1945 - 1949 | 1949 - 1953 |
|---|---|
| ➢ **UNITED NATIONS** - first meeting. | ➢ **UNDERDOG TRUMAN STUNS NATION - WINS RE-ELECTION** |
| ➢ **V-E DAY** - Germany surrenders. | |
| ➢ **U.S. DROPS ATOM BOMBS ON HIROSHIMA AND NAGASAKI** | ➢ **FAIR DEAL** - guarantees collective bargaining, repeals Taft-Hartley law, increased minimum wage, price support for farms, improved housing. |
| ➢ **V-J DAY** - Japan surrenders. | |
| ➢ **YALTA CONFERENCE** - Roosevelt, Churchill and Stalin plan the peace strategy after World War II. (298,000 Americans killed). | ➢ **NORTH ATLANTIC TREATY ORG.** - U.S. troops are still in Europe today. |
| | ➢ **COMMUNIST NORTH KOREA INVADES SOUTH KOREA** |
| ➢ **ROOSEVELT ARRANGES DEAL WITH SAUDI ARABIA** - to provide U.S. protection in exchange for access to oil, primarily to ensure Europe's ability to rebuild after World War II. | ➢ **TRUMAN SENDS U.S. GROUND TROOPS TO ASSIST SOUTH KOREA** - U.S. troops are still in S. Korea today. |
| | ➢ **TRUMAN FIRES GENERAL MACARTHUR** |
| ➢ **FRANKLIN D. ROOSEVELT DIES** - V.P. Truman becomes president. | ➢ **TRUMAN IMPOSES WAGE & PRICE CONTROLS** |
| ➢ **FULL EMPLOYMENT ACT** | ➢ **JOE MCCARTHY EPISODE** (Communist infiltration scare). |
| ➢ **"IRON CURTAIN"** - describes the division between the USSR & West. | |
| | ➢ **22ND AMENDMENT** - limits Presidents to two, four-year terms. |
| ➢ **MARSHALL PLAN** - rebuilds Europe. | |
| ➢ **ISRAEL** - declared a nation. | ➢ **TRUMAN FIRST U.S. PRESIDENT TO PROPOSE NATIONAL HEALTHCARE** |
| ➢ **BERLIN AIRLIFT** | |

| HOUSE MAJORITY | | | |
|---|---|---|---|
| DEM — 242 | REP — 246 | DEM — 263 | DEM — 235 |
| **SENATE MAJORITY** | | | |
| DEM — 57 | REP — 51 | DEM — 54 | DEM — 49 |
| **79th Congress** | **80th Congress** | **81st Congress** | **82nd Congress** |
| **HOUSE MINORITY** | | | |
| REP — 191 | DEM — 188 | REP — 171 | REP — 199 |
| **SENATE MINORITY** | | | |
| REP — 38 | DEM — 45 | REP — 42 | REP — 47 |

# Dwight David Eisenhower

34th President
(1953 - 1961)
Republican

| 1953 - 1957 | 1957 - 1961 |
|---|---|
| ➤ WAGE CONTROLS ABOLISHED | ➤ EISENHOWER DOCTRINE - U.S. to provide military and financial aid to any country in the middle-east to prevent communist aggression. |
| ➤ DEPARTMENT OF HEALTH, EDUCATION & WELFARE (HEW) | |
| ➤ KOREAN WAR ENDS - demilitarized zone established (150,000 American casualties.) | ➤ CIVIL RIGHTS ACT OF 1957 - CIVIL RIGHTS COMMISSION |
| ➤ ST. LAWRENCE SEAWAY - U.S. & Canadian construction links the Great Lakes to the St. Lawrence Estuary - one of world's most comprehensive inland navigation systems (an expandable project.) | ➤ LITTLE ROCK CENTRAL HIGH SCHOOL - Arkansas governor Orville Faubus orders National Guard to prevent the admission of black children. |
| | ➤ FEDERAL COURT ORDERS THAT THE STUDENTS BE ADMITTED - Arkansas then closes the school. |
| ➤ BROWN VS. TOPEKA - Supreme court declares racial separation of public schools unconstitutional. | ➤ EISENHOWER DEPLOYS FEDERAL TROOPS TO RE-OPEN THE SCHOOL |
| ➤ FIRST ATOMIC SUBMARINE LAUNCHED - U.S. *NAUTILUS* | ➤ SOVIET UNION LAUNCHES SPUTNIK - First satellite to orbit earth. |
| ➤ EISENHOWER VETOS NATIONAL GAS ACT | ➤ FIDEL CASTRO BECOMES CUBAN LEADER |
| ➤ WEST GERMANY RECOGNIZED AS AN INDEPENDENT COUNTRY | ➤ U.S. U-2 RECONNAISSANCE PLANE SHOT DOWN OVER SOVIET UNION |
| ➤ JULIUS & ETHEL ROSENBURG - sentenced to death for supplying atomic data to Soviet Union. | ➤ ALASKA & HAWAII ADMITTED AS 49TH & 50TH STATES |

| HOUSE MAJORITY | | | |
|---|---|---|---|
| REP — 221 | DEM — 232 | DEM — 234 | DEM — 283 |
| SENATE MAJORITY | | | |
| REP — 48 | DEM — 48 | DEM — 49 | DEM — 65 |
| 83rd Congress | 84th Congress | 85th Congress | 86th Congress |
| HOUSE MINORITY | | | |
| DEM — 213 | REP — 203 | REP — 201 | REP — 153 |
| SENATE MINORITY | | | |
| DEM — 47 | REP — 47 | REP — 478 | REP — 35 |

| John Fitzgerald Kennedy | Lyndon Baines Johnson |
|---|---|
| 35th President<br>(1961 - 1963)<br>Democrat | 36th President<br>(1963 - 1969)<br>Democrat |
| **1961 - 1965** | **1965 - 1969** |

**John Fitzgerald Kennedy (1961 - 1965)**

- ➢ **KENNEDY CAMPAIGNS FOR MEDICARE**

- ➢ **PEACE CORPS**

- ➢ **BAY OF PIGS INVASION** - 1,400 anti-Castro cuban exiles (trained by the CIA) invade Cuba but are defeated because U.S. reinforcements were cancelled.

- ➢ **KENNEDY SECURES FUNDING FOR THE APOLLO MOON LAUNCH**

- ➢ **CUBAN MISSILE CRISIS** - after the discovery of Russian offensive missiles in Cuba, the U.S. set up a naval "quarantine" of Cuba. Soviet ships refused to challenge the "quarantine" and war was avoided.

- ➢ **CIVIL RIGHTS MARCH IN WASHINGTON, D.C.** - Martin Luther King, Jr. leads 200,000 to demonstrate for "jobs & freedom."

- ➢ **KENNEDY PROPOSES TAX CUTS TO BOOST ECONOMY**

- ➢ **KENNEDY ASSASSINATED - V.P. JOHNSON BECOMES PRESIDENT**

**Lyndon Baines Johnson (1965 - 1969)**

- ➢ WAR DECLARED ON POVERTY

- ➢ WAR IN VIETNAM ESCALATES

- ➢ *THE GREAT SOCIETY* PROGRAMS

- ➢ ECONOMIC OPPORTUNITY ACT

- ➢ MEDICARE ACT

- ➢ VOTING RIGHTS ACT

- ➢ DEPARTMENT OF HOUSING & URBAN DEVELOPMENT

- ➢ HIGHER EDUCATION ACT

- ➢ DEPARTMENT OF TRANSPORTATION ESTABLISHED

- ➢ CLEAN WATER RESTORATION ACT

- ➢ CIVIL RIGHTS ACT

- ➢ FEDERAL WATER SUPPLY BILL

- ➢ CONSERVATION & BEAUTIFICATION ACT

- ➢ ANTI-VIETNAM WAR RALLIES

- ➢ MARTIN L. KING JR. ASSASSINATED

- ➢ ROBERT KENNEDY ASSASSINATED

- ➢ VIETNAM RAGES ON

- ➢ JOHNSON RETIRES

| HOUSE MAJORITY | | | |
|---|---|---|---|
| DEM — 263 | DEM — 259 | DEM — 295 | DEM — 247 |
| **SENATE MAJORITY** | | | |
| DEM — 64 | DEM — 66 | DEM — 68 | DEM — 64 |
| **87th Congress** | **88th Congress** | **89th Congress** | **90th Congress** |
| **HOUSE MINORITY** | | | |
| REP — 174 | REP — 176 | REP — 140 | REP — 187 |
| **SENATE MINORITY** | | | |
| REP — 36 | REP — 34 | REP — 32 | REP — 36 |

| Richard Milhous Nixon | Gerald Rudolph Ford |
|---|---|
| 37th President<br>(1969 - 1974)<br>Republican | 38th President<br>(1974 - 1977)<br>Republican |
| **1969 - 1973** | **1973 - 1977** |

| | |
|---|---|
| ➢ **APOLLO MOON LANDING -** Kennedy's agenda completed. | ➢ **ARAB OIL EMBARGO -** protesting American support of Israel. |
| ➢ **SUPREME COURT DECLARES SCHOOL DESEGREGATION** | ➢ **FEDERAL ENERGY ADMINISTRATION** |
| ➢ **KENT STATE UNIVERSITY -** four students killed by Ohio National Guard at anti-war rally. | ➢ **NATIONAL HEALTH INSURANCE PROPOSED - CHIP** (Comprehensive Health Insurance Plan) "An idea whose time has come in America." |
| ➢ **U.S. GROUND TROOPS DEPLOYED TO CAMBODIA** | ➢ **NIXON'S PRESS CONFERENCE -** "I have never obstructed justice ... I am not a crook." |
| ➢ **ALL U.S. GROUND TROOPS WITHDRAWN FROM VIETNAM -** (50,000 Americans died.) | ➢ **NIXON'S IMPEACHMENT HEARINGS** |
| | ➢ **NIXON RESIGNS FROM OFFICE** |
| ➢ **EQUAL RIGHTS PROPOSAL -** would ban gender discrimination. | ➢ **V.P. FORD BECOMES PRESIDENT** |
| ➢ **NIXON OPENS THE DOOR TO CHINA** | ➢ **PRESIDENT FORD PARDONS NIXON** |
| ➢ **ENVIRONMENTAL PROTECTION AGENCY (EPA)** | ➢ **FREEDOM OF INFORMATION ACT** |
| ➢ **WAGE & PRICE FREEZE** | ➢ **PUBLIC FUNDING FOR PRESIDENTIAL CAMPAIGNS** |
| ➢ **DOLLAR REMOVED FROM GOLD STANDARD** | ➢ **FORD PROPOSES NATIONAL HEALTH INSURANCE** |
| ➢ **BREAK IN AT WATERGATE** | ➢ **OPEC INCREASES PRICE OF OIL 10%** |
| | ➢ **FORD PROPOSES STRINGENT ENERGY POLICY** |

| HOUSE MAJORITY | | | |
|---|---|---|---|
| DEM — 243 | DEM — 255 | DEM — 242 | DEM — 291 |
| **SENATE MAJORITY** | | | |
| DEM — 57 | DEM — 54 | DEM — 56 | DEM — 60 |
| **91st Congress** | **92nd Congress** | **93rd Congress** | **94th Congress** |
| **HOUSE MINORITY** | | | |
| REP — 192 | REP — 180 | REP — 192 | REP — 144 |
| **SENATE MINORITY** | | | |
| REP — 43 | REP — 44 | REP — 42 | REP — 38 |

| James Earl Carter | Ronald Wilson Reagan |
|---|---|
| 39th President<br>(1977 - 1981)<br>Democrat | 40th President<br>(1981 - 1989)<br>Republican |
| **1977 - 1981** | **1981 - 1985** |

| | |
|---|---|
| ➢ PANAMA CANAL TREATY<br><br>➢ LARGEST U.S. TRADE DEFICIT<br><br>➢ OPEC INCREASES PRICE OF OIL 14%<br>- gas rationing & shortages in U.S.<br><br>➢ CARTER PROPOSES COMPREHENSIVE ENERGY PROGRAM<br><br>➢ DEPARTMENT OF EDUCATION<br><br>➢ CARTER PROPOSES NATIONAL HEALTH INSURANCE<br><br>➢ IRANIAN HOSTAGE CRISIS<br><br>➢ SOVIET UNION INVADES AFGHANISTAN<br><br>➢ "MISERY INDEX" - measures U.S. economy.<br>• CONSUMER PRICE INDEX 13%<br>• UNEMPLOYMENT 12%<br>• MORTGAGE RATES 18%<br><br>➢ CONGRESS OVERRIDES CARTER'S VETO - a bill that would have imposed a fee on imported oil. First override in 28 years of a President of a majority party! | ➢ U.S. HOSTAGES RELEASED FROM IRAN<br><br>➢ REAGAN REJECTS THE SALT TREATY WITH RUSSIANS<br><br>➢ REAGAN SHOT BY JOHN HINCKLEY<br><br>➢ SANDRA DAY O'CONNOR - first woman supreme court justice.<br><br>➢ "REAGANOMICS" - $750 BILLION IN TAX CUTS TO STIMULATE THE ECONOMY<br><br>➢ REAGAN FIRES 13,000 AIR TRAFFIC CONTROLLERS<br><br>➢ REAGAN CALLS THE SOVIET UNION AN "EVIL EMPIRE"<br><br>➢ ISRAEL INVADES LEBANON<br><br>➢ U.S. MARINE HEADQUARTERS BOMBED BY MUSLIM TERRORISTS IN BEIRUT, LEBANON<br><br>➢ DEFICIT REDUCTION ACT<br><br>➢ STRATEGIC DEFENSE INITIATIVE "STAR WARS" - Defensive Missile Shield - Russians can't compete. |

| HOUSE MAJORITY | | | |
|---|---|---|---|
| DEM — 292 | DEM — 277 | DEM — 242 | DEM — 269 |

| SENATE MAJORITY | | | |
|---|---|---|---|
| DEM — 61 | DEM — 58 | REP — 53 | REP — 54 |

| 95th Congress | 96th Congress | 97th Congress | 98th Congress |
|---|---|---|---|

| HOUSE MINORITY | | | |
|---|---|---|---|
| REP — 143 | REP — 158 | REP — 192 | REP — 166 |

| SENATE MINORITY | | | |
|---|---|---|---|
| REP — 38 | REP — 41 | DEM — 46 | DEM — 46 |

| Ronald Wilson Reagan | George Herbert Walker Bush |
|---|---|
| 40th President<br>(1981 - 1989)<br>Republican | 41st President<br>(1989 - 1993)<br>Republican |
| **1985 - 1989** | **1989 - 1993** |

| | |
|---|---|
| ➤ **GRAMM-RUDMAN BILL** - 5 year plan to end deficit.<br><br>➤ **IRAQI MISSILE KILLS 37 SAILORS ON A FRIGATE IN THE PERSIAN GULF**<br><br>➤ **TAX REFORM ACT OF 1986** - most comprehensive revision of tax code in more than 40 years, lowering taxes.<br><br>➤ **"BLACK MONDAY" OCTOBER 19, 1987 - STOCK MARKET LOSES 25% IN ONE DAY!**<br><br>➤ **U.S. CONDUCTS AIR RAIDS ON LIBYA TO DETER ADDITIONAL TERRORIST STRIKES**<br><br>➤ **IMMIGRATION REFORM AND CONTROL ACT** - prohibits employers from hiring illegal immigrants.<br><br>➤ **NEUTRALITY ACT** - attempt to avoid U.S. involvement in World Wars.<br><br>➤ **REAGAN REJECTS MISSILE TREATY WITH GORBACHEV IN ICELAND**<br><br>  • Media & Liberals outraged & refer to Reagan as "Ronald Ray Gun"<br><br>  • Tipping Point for the eventual implosion of the Soviet Union | ➤ **EXXON'S VALDEZ OIL SPILL FOULS 730 MILES OF ALASKAN COASTLINE** - 400,000 animals killed.<br><br>➤ **CHINA KILLS HUNDREDS OF STUDENTS & DEMONSTRATORS WHO WERE MAKING A PEACEFUL STATEMENT ABOUT DEMOCRACY IN TIANANMEN SQUARE**<br><br>➤ **AMERICANS WITH DISABILITIES ACT**<br><br>➤ **BUSH REVERSES TAX POSITION** - ("Read my Lips … No New Taxes") raises taxes $140 Billion - economy soon goes into a recession!<br><br>➤ **CLEAN AIR ACT**<br><br>➤ **IMMIGRATION ACT OF 1990** - limits total number of immigrants to 700,000 per year.<br><br>➤ **OPERATION DESERT STORM** - Bush leads a large coalition of nations to oust Saddam Hussein out of Kuwait.<br><br>➤ **MIKHAIL GORBACHEV RESIGNS - SOVIET UNION DISSOLVES**<br><br>➤ **ROE V. WADE** - Supreme court gives women the right to abortion. |

| HOUSE MAJORITY | | | |
|---|---|---|---|
| DEM — 253 | DEM — 258 | DEM — 260 | DEM — 267 |
| SENATE MAJORITY | | | |
| REP — 53 | DEM — 55 | DEM — 55 | DEM — 56 |
| 99th<br>Congress | 100th<br>Congress | 101st<br>Congress | 102nd<br>Congress |
| HOUSE MINORITY | | | |
| REP — 182 | REP — 177 | REP — 175 | REP — 167 |
| SENATE MINORITY | | | |
| DEM — 47 | REP — 45 | REP — 45 | REP — 44 |

# William Jefferson Clinton

## 42nd President
## (1993 - 2001)
## Democrat

| 1993 - 1997 | 1997 - 2001 |
|---|---|
| ➢ HILLARY CLINTON APPOINTED TO CHAIR TASK FORCE FOR A NATIONAL HEALTHCARE SYSTEM<br><br>➢ FAMILY & MEDICAL LEAVE ACT<br><br>➢ TERRORISTS EXPLODE BOMB AT THE WORLD TRADE CENTER - American response was the use of civil courts.<br><br>➢ OMNIBUS BUDGET RECONCILIATION ACT - to reduce federal budget deficit by cutting spending & raising taxes by $241 Billion.<br><br>➢ NORTH AMERICAN FREE TRADE AGREEMENT (NAFTA) - Mexico, U.S. & Canada now the world's largest free trade zone.<br><br>➢ PAULA JONES FILES LAWSUIT AGAINST CLINTON FOR SEXUAL HARASSMENT<br><br>➢ HILLARY CLINTON TESTIFIES AT FEDERAL GRAND JURY - concerning Whitewater development deal.<br><br>➢ HEALTHCARE PROPOSAL FAILS<br><br>➢ REPUBLICANS GAIN CONTROL OF THE HOUSE & THE SENATE - FIRST TIME IN 40 YEARS! | ➢ SENATE GOVT. AFFAIRS COMMITTEE - reports numerous campaign fund-raising abuses - including China's attempt to make illegal contributions to Clinton's campaign. Johnny Chung (democratic fund-raiser) pleads guilty.<br><br>➢ 1ST BALANCED BUDGET IN 30 YRS<br><br>➢ CLINTON PAYS PAULA JONES - $850,000 settles harassment case.<br><br>➢ CLINTON HELD IN CONTEMPT - for false testimony in Paula Jones case.<br><br>➢ ISLAMIC TERRORISTS RAM U.S.S. *COLE* - (17 Americans killed.)<br><br>➢ TRADE WITH CHINA NORMALIZED<br><br>➢ NATO BOMBS BELGRADE - to force Serbians to cease attacking Albanian Muslims in Kosovo.<br><br>➢ MONICA LEWINSKY SCANDAL - Clinton denies and later confesses to an affair with a young White House intern.<br><br>➢ ECONOMIC COLLAPSE - STOCK MARKET BEGINS 3 YEAR TUMBLE - TECH STOCK BUBBLE BURSTS - last year of the Clinton administration is the first year of a three year recession. |

| HOUSE MAJORITY | | | |
|---|---|---|---|
| DEM — 258 | REP — 230 | REP — 228 | REP — 223 |
| **SENATE MAJORITY** | | | |
| DEM — 57 | REP — 52 | REP — 55 | REP — 55 |
| 103rd Congress | 104th Congress | 105th Congress | 106th Congress |
| **HOUSE MINORITY** | | | |
| REP — 176 | DEM — 204 | DEM — 206 | DEM — 211 |
| **SENATE MINORITY** | | | |
| REP — 43 | DEM — 48 | DEM — 45 | DEM — 45 |

# George Walker Bush

43rd President
(2001 - 2009)
Republican

| 2001 - 2005 | 2005 - 2009 |
|---|---|
| ➢ 2ND & 3RD YEAR OF RECESSION | ➢ ISLAMIC TERRORISTS BOMB MADRID TRAIN STATION - nearly 200 killed. |
| ➢ BUSH ENACTS $1.35 TRILLION TAX-CUT BILL TO STIMULATE THE RECESSION RIDDLED ECONOMY | ➢ 200,000 KILLED IN INDONESIA BY A DEADLY TSUNAMI |
| ➢ FINANCE REFORM BILL - limits campaign contributions. | ➢ 11 MILLION ILLEGAL IMMIGRANTS CAUSE HOSTILE REACTIONS IN U.S. |
| ➢ BUSH WARNS SADDAM HUSSEIN TO COMPLY WITH U.N. RESOLUTION AGAINST BIOLOGICAL WEAPONS ON JANUARY 22, 2001 | ➢ THE PRICE OF OIL ROCKETS TO OVER $140 A BARREL |
| | ➢ GASOLINE APPROACHES $5 A GALLON |
| ➢ 9/11/2001 - MUSLIM TERRORISTS DESTROY WORLD TRADE CENTER - 3,000 KILLED | ➢ INFLATION REIGNITES |
| ➢ ENRON FILES FOR BANKRUPTCY | ➢ REAL ESTATE PRICES PLUMMET |
| ➢ NO CHILD LEFT BEHIND ACT | ➢ STOCK MARKET PRICES AT 1999 LEVELS |
| ➢ U.S. INVADES IRAQ | ➢ VALUE OF THE DOLLAR PERILOUSLY LOW |
| ➢ U.S. CAPTURES SADDAM HUSSEIN | |
| ➢ PATRIOT ACT - increased wiretapping & surveillance. | ➢ BUDGET & TRADE DEFICITS EXPANDING DANGEROUSLY |
| ➢ HOMELAND SECURITY BILL - protection against terrorism. | ➢ MIDDLE OF AMERICA FLOODED WHILE OTHER AREAS SUFFER DROUGHT - America still lacks a National Water Control System. |

| HOUSE MAJORITY | | | |
|---|---|---|---|
| REP — 221 | REP — 229 | REP — 232 | DEM — 233 |

| SENATE MAJORITY | | | |
|---|---|---|---|
| DEM — 50 | REP — 51 | REP — 55 | DEM — 50 |

| 107th Congress | 108th Congress | 109th Congress | 110th Congress |
|---|---|---|---|

| HOUSE MINORITY | | | |
|---|---|---|---|
| DEM — 212 | DEM — 204 | DEM — 202 | REP — 202 |

| SENATE MINORITY | | | |
|---|---|---|---|
| REP — 49 | DEM — 48 | DEM — 44 | REP — 49 |

## CHAPTER TWO

# PRESIDENT JOHN F. KENNEDY 1961 - 1963
# &
# THE
# APOLLO SPACE PROGRAM

# AN
# OPPORTUNITY SEIZED!

*Some men see things as they are and say, "why?"*
*I dream things that never were and say "why not?"*

— GEORGE BERNARD SHAW

# THE PROBLEM

*"Now, so far as the satellite itself is concerned,*
*one small ball in the air, that does*
*not raise my apprehensions, not one iota.*
*I see nothing at this moment ...*
*that is significant in that development*
*as far as security is concerned."*

— PRESIDENT EISENHOWER'S REACTION IN 1957, TO THE RUSSIAN'S LAUNCH OF SPUTNIK, THE FIRST SATELLITE TO ORBIT THE EARTH.[1]

Fortunately, the fact that the Russians could put heavy objects in orbit that could pass over the United States did send off alarm bells for other more perceptive Americans. Senator John Kennedy and, to an even greater extent, Senator Lyndon Johnson, understood that the same basic physics that propelled a satellite could also apply to armed nuclear weapons. Like many other military men, President Eisenhower understood the potential of a new war only through the lens of the weaponry of the last war.

Two months later on December 6, 1957, the first full-scale U.S. Vanguard test satellite blew up seconds after lift-off. Americans — and the rest of the world — realized that the Russian's space technology was far superior to that of

36

the U.S. This was a critical problem for multiple reasons. The political and military advantage of our cold war enemy was a threatening prospect.

However, the greater threat was that the citizens in dozens of other countries would conclude that communist socialism was superior to a free capitalistic society. At that time, the Soviet Union and the United States were both competing for the hearts and minds of people in many other countries. If America became an island of freedom isolated in an ocean of communist countries, its future would become very bleak indeed.

America's initial leader in the space race was Senate Majority Leader, Lyndon Johnson. More than anyone, he understood both the gravity of the situation and the political opportunity. On November 25, 1957, he chaired the first meeting of the Senate Preparedness Investigation Subcommittee of the Senate Armed Services Committee.

The following summer, the legislative framework for the space program evolved after passage of the National Space Act. Despite what might have appeared as a forward push by the Eisenhower administration, the clear fact was that the president did not support the space effort. Johnson's accomplishments were made in spite of the president's passive resistance. Eisenhower's

EISENHOWER'S LAST ACT IN DECEMBER OF 1960 WAS TO TURN DOWN NASA'S REQUESTS FOR FLIGHTS AROUND AND TO THE MOON.

last act in December of 1960 was to turn down NASA's requests for flights around and to the moon.[2]

Eisenhower considered increased military spending, which to him included space programs, to be a direct reduction in America's ability to tend to human needs. "Every gun that is fired, every warship launched, every rocket fired signifies ... a theft from those who hunger and are not fed, those who are cold and are not clothed."[3] Not only was his philosophy about government spending an obstacle to his support of space initiatives, but he also harbored serious concerns about the potential dangers of an unchecked and out of control military/arms industry. In his farewell address on January 18, 1961, he warned:

> *Our military organization today bears little relation to that known by any of my predecessors in peacetime ...*

> *The conjunction of an immense military establishment and a large arms industry is new in the American experience. The total influence — economic, political, even spiritual — is felt in every city, every State house, every office of the federal government. We recognize the imperative need for this development. Yet we must not fail to comprehend its grave implications ...*

> *In the councils of government, we must guard against the acquisition of unwarranted influence, whether sought or unsought, by the military/industrial complex. The*

*potential for the disastrous rise of misplaced power exists and will persist.*

*We must never let the weight of this combination endanger our liberties or democratic processes. We should take nothing for granted. Only an alert and knowledgeable citizenry can compel the proper meshing of the huge industrial and military machinery of defense with our peaceful methods and goals.*

His concerns were unquestionably warranted, as time would later confirm. However, the last few years of Eisenhower's presidency also included a chapter of American history that was fraught with fear and danger. In the late 1950's, school children (including this writer) routinely practiced huddling under their desks in case of a nuclear attack by the Soviet Union. "Fallout shelters" were purchased by many homeowners across the country who hoped to survive a massive assault. The threats were real, and many Americans were living in a constant state of high anxiety.

THE THREATS WERE REAL, AND MANY AMERICANS WERE LIVING IN A CONSTANT STATE OF HIGH ANXIETY.

International events made a bad situation even worse. One of the U.S. spy planes that the Eisenhower administration had denied even existed was shot down over Soviet air space on May 1, 1960, and U-2 pilot Gary Powers was captured.[4]   The Russians' reaction was predictable, but they were further angered when President Eisenhower refused to apologize to Premier Khrushchev at a subsequent meeting in Paris.  The Cold War had become even more intense.  The whole world was watching and Americans were now living in constant fear of annihilation.

## THE 1960 PRESIDENTIAL CAMPAIGN

As the 1960 presidential campaign got under way, Lyndon Johnson and John Kennedy battled for the democratic nomination.  Both candidates campaigned on a platform that included a significant space initiative to counter the Russians' superiority.  As a campaigner, JFK also understood the importance of building a popular base of support for what would be one of his major agenda items should he become the next president.

Even though the campaign struggle left some bad feelings in both camps, Kennedy, who received the nomination at the convention, knew the value of having Johnson as a running mate.  Not only could Lyndon deliver Texas in the November election, but as the Senate Majority Leader and the leading proponent of the space program, he would be invaluable after the election as well.  Kennedy understood the necessity of assembling a capable legislative team that could navigate Washington politics.

During the campaign, Kennedy strongly and repeatedly criticized Eisenhower for lack of vision, understanding, and effort in regard to the Soviet space threat. For example, in one speech in 1960, he warned of the consequences of not understanding the seriousness of the situation.

*If the Soviet Union was first in outer space, that is the most serious defeat the United States has suffered in many, many years ... Because we failed to recognize the impact that being first in outer space would have, the impression began to move around the world that the Soviet Union was on the march, that it had definite goals, that it knew how to accomplish them, that it was moving and we were standing still. That is what we have to overcome, the psychological feeling in the world that the United States has reached maturity, that maybe our high noon has passed ... and that now we are going into the long, slow afternoon.[5]*

On October 10, 1960, just weeks before the November election, Kennedy continued to make his case in a way that would lay down a foundation of public support for his presidential space agenda:

*"We are in a strategic space race with the Russians, and we are losing ... To insure peace and freedom, we must be first. This is the new age of exploration; space is our great New Frontier."[6]*

41

As a presidential candidate, Kennedy promised to "outdo" the Russians in the "first 90 days" in office.[7] Hammering away relentlessly at the "space gap" and the "missile gap," he made it quite clear to the voters that (A) America had a serious problem, and (B) if elected, he was going to do something about it — quickly!

Aided by the new technology of television, a tanned and photogenic Kennedy "won" the first televised presidential debates. However, polls showed that a majority of the people who had listened to the radio thought that Richard Nixon was the clear winner. Kennedy won the 1960 presidential election by a razor thin margin. However, America and the world were about to experience a distinctly different style of leadership than that of Eisenhower's passive guardianship of the status quo.

Kennedy was a man who saw a better future ahead, and he spoke in terms that would elevate Americans to think of greater possibilities and of greater personal responsibility. The famous lines from his inaugural speech "Ask not what your country can do for you — ask what you can do for your country" are familiar to nearly all Americans (even if they cannot remember who said it).[8]

## A New President & A New Agenda

In that speech given on a cold day in January 1960, Kennedy also laid the ground work for bold initiatives that would breathe life into part of his vision of The *New Frontier:*

*Let every nation know, whether it wishes us well or ill, that we shall pay any price, bear any burden, meet any hardship, support any friend, oppose any foe to assure the survival and the success of liberty. For only when our arms are sufficient beyond doubt can we be certain beyond doubt that they will never be used.*[9]

The peace through strength doctrine was now established — but its definition was a blank slate for the new president. It would include sending a man to the moon!

Kennedy brought many changes to the White House. Outwardly, youth and vigor were apparent. As the new first lady, Jackie's sophisticated charm and beauty added a fresh look. Presidential toddlers and presidential football games on the white house lawn, along with eloquent oratory that appealed to the American people's higher sense of purpose and destiny, offered a sharp contrast to the Eisenhower years. Inside the new administration, other changes were also underway.

THE PEACE THROUGH STRENGTH DOCTRINE WAS NOW ESTABLISHED — BUT ITS DEFINITION WAS A BLANK SLATE FOR THE NEW PRESIDENT. IT WOULD INCLUDE SENDING A MAN TO THE MOON!

The *New Frontier* would include an ambitious legislative agenda. Although hoping to expand on FDR's *New Deal*, Kennedy astutely knew that it would be an uphill battle. Even though the Democrats held a majority in the House and the Senate, for years their southern delegation, the "Dixiecrats," had usually voted with the Republicans, especially on racial issues and government spending.

It had been (and would continue to be) the southern democratic governors who fought integration at the local level and the southern democratic senators and congressional representatives who would fight it at the federal level. Kennedy knew that building a coalition of a majority of the Congress would be one of his biggest challenges. Fortunately, the newly designed but unused blueprint for coalition building created by President Eisenhower's staff was left behind for the new administration.

## LAWRENCE O'BRIEN & THE OCR

Until that time, there was not a specific person or position whose job it was to successfully get the president's agenda through Congress. While the organizational concept was initiated by Eisenhower, it was ultimately Kennedy who gave it life. Lawrence O'Brien had been a major player in the Kennedy campaign as an organizer, tireless worker, and the "do whatever it takes" person who made things happen. He was the obvious choice to head up the congressional liaison.

O'Brien's design and operation of the Office of Congressional Relations (OCR) would become the prototype for future administrations. It took time and a learning curve before the OCR was an effective legislative tool. In fact, the OCR (and O'Brien) would not finally hit its stride until a few years later in the Johnson administration. However, even in its "learning to walk" early stages, the OCR began to have an impact.

Today, setting up a detailed folder on every legislator seems to be an obvious thing to do yet it had never been done before O'Brien began to organize the legislative process. David Bell, the Director of the Budget noted, "The O'Brien office provided the president a continuous flow of information on how the people in the Congress were feeling about current issues and about different matters."[10]

In sports, successful coaches usually scout the teams that they will go up against. Kennedy grasped that basic concept and instructed O'Brien to get as much useful information as possible on each of the legislators.

The file on Representative Frank Ikard (D-Texas) was a classic example of O'Brien's handiwork. A small picture of the congressman was stapled in the top right corner along with the phonetic spelling (eye-cord) of his name. The "Biographical" section included details of his family and history. Under "Personal," O'Brien noted that a "Texas contact" said, "Ikard is ruled by three forces." The first was "a wealthy Texas oil and blooded cattleman named J.S. Bridwell." The second was "newspaper owner, Rhea Howard." The third major influence was the Texas Independent Petroleum and Royalty Owners Association.[11]

The "Political Fealty" section stated that Ikard usually

followed the lead of Sam Rayburn, Lyndon Johnson and the oil interests. It noted that even though he voted with the Democratic Party 81% of the time, he also voted with the "conservative coalition" on 57% of the roll calls in the 86th Congress.[12] The file suggested to Kennedy that Ikard would not be supportive of his liberal *New Frontier* agenda.

A similar assessment of all the legislators provided Kennedy with a fairly accurate picture of his current political strengths as well as the ability to prioritize his potential converts by their historical voting patterns. By knowing the identity of people who could influence their thinking, he could ultimately influence legislator votes.

... "NOWHERE WILL THE GAME BE PLAYED MORE OPENLY THAN IN THE SECOND-FLOOR WHITE HOUSE OFFICE OF LARRY O'BRIEN."

O'Brien also perfected the art of patronage. In the everyday world of political give and take, the Kennedy administration used every perk of the presidency to accumulate votes one at a time. O'Brien was identified by both Newsweek and the New York Times as the president's patronage chief. Time magazine wrote, "Nowhere will the game be played more openly than in the second-floor White House office of Larry O'Brien."[13]

A pet tool of O'Brien's was to retain complete control of the disbursement of the tickets for tours of the White House. Congressional representatives would need to go through O'Brien's office in order to supply their constituents with tour tickets. By deliberately delaying the requests, it would many times put a congressman in the compromising position of having to agree to something (usually a vote) in order to get the tickets and thus not disappoint the visitors from his home state.

If the congressman was a Kennedy (or later a Johnson) supporter, the delivery of tour passes was accompanied by an explanation of how they (OCR) had just done the impossible for the congressman because there were no more passes available for that day. The unspoken message was that if the congressman wanted to be able to get tickets on short notice again, he or she should support the administration. On many occasions, legislators who were considered foes were unable to secure tour passes unless they were requested far in advance.

The most powerful use of patronage came through the Executive Branch departments. Deliberately backing certain federal projects and the eventual choice of which companies would be given the resulting contracts offered the administration an excellent opportunity to line up support for other issues in exchange for the awards. Before the cabinet members who would be making those calls were chosen, O'Brien interviewed them and explained:

*"There would be but one Administration legislative program — the president's; that we were all to be part of one team and would maintain close contact; that major*

*appointments would be cleared by the White House; and that we should not forget we had another election coming up in 1964."* [14]

These traditional aspects of presidential leadership were just as important and necessary in accumulating congressional votes as were Kennedy's inspiring oratories that stirred the hearts and souls of some of the other members of the House and Senate. The adage "Different strokes for different folks" describes the need of a president to appeal to various people based upon their particular needs or personal motivations.

The young president quickly learned the ropes of Washington's presidential politics. The ability to assemble a majority vote is the minimum threshold for passing any legislation. Unfortunately, many presidents fail to comprehend that most basic and fundamental concept. Kennedy was not one of them!

## RUSSIAN SUPERIORITY IN SPACE

Before even a hundred days had passed since his eloquent and moving inaugural speech in January 1961, the Russians gave Kennedy (and the world) a mega-dose of communist reality. On April 12, 1961, Russian cosmonaut Yuri Gargarin became the first man to orbit the earth. The world's first space ship, Vostok, carried him as a passenger (he did not pilot the craft) for 89 minutes about 200 miles above the earth.

The Soviet propaganda machine went to work overtime. Khrushchev bellowed, "Let the capitalist countries catch up with our country." Ulbricht, the East German leader, said that the orbit "demonstrates to the whole world that socialism must triumph over the decaying system of yesterday." The Central Committee of the Communist Party claimed that in this achievement "are embodied the genius of the Soviet people and the powerful force of socialism."[15]

In early 1961, many other non-aligned countries saw no reason to disagree. Kennedy knew that a crisis demanded a quick response and that the energy of a crisis, if properly channeled, could be a tremendous tool in breaking up the normal political logjams. He would seize the opportunity.

---

*"The people who get on in this world are the people who get up and look for the circumstances they want, and, if they can't find them, make them."*

— GEORGE BERNARD SHAW

---

Kennedy asked his trusted advisor Ted Sorenson to give him a list of all of the feasible projects that, if accomplished, could regain America's real and perceived technological dominance. The discussions included ideas such as "desalting" [sic] the oceans. However, it was quickly surmised that a space achievement was the only viable option. It was also determined that the Russians were already far ahead in any project that would be attainable within a few years.

## LET'S GO TO THE MOON!

The idea of sending a man to the moon within a decade would provide America with the greatest possible technological demonstration for the world to witness. A spectacular display of scientific achievement would undoubtedly make the case to the world that a free and capitalistic society was the type of system that other countries should adopt. It also provided enough time for the U.S. to actually pull ahead of the Russian capabilities and eventually score a clear victory.

There were several additional distinct advantages in setting both a distant and specific time frame for the moon launch. If Kennedy audaciously announced to the world our bold intentions to send a man to the moon, America would be able to reap a propaganda bonanza for many years — even before we actually reached our goal.

There would be an assumption by many observers around the world that if we were confident enough to publicly declare our grand intentions, then we must have the capability to pull it off. We could appear to be winning the space race even before we actually caught up with the Russians.

Another critical advantage of setting a specific time frame was the self-imposed dynamic of working toward a deadline. While this tool is usually present in our personal lives as well as for the companies that employ most Americans, it is usually glaringly absent in government work.

> WE COULD APPEAR TO BE WINNING THE SPACE RACE EVEN BEFORE WE ACTUALLY CAUGHT UP WITH THE RUSSIANS.

Nearly anyone who has ever watched a football game understands that as the time remaining continues to diminish, its effect on the players continues to increase. The players' focus and concentration during the last two minutes of the game (especially if it is a close game and one that really counts — like a space race with the Russians) is significantly more intense than it was during the first quarter.

If we are driving to work and we may not make it on time, our focus is much greater than if we were merely driving to the grocery store. Deadlines are powerful tools if used wisely.

Though he had only been president for a few months, Kennedy was ready to grab a bat, walk up to the plate, and attempt to hit a home run. Like Babe Ruth, who once famously pointed to a place in the stands where he intended to hit a home run — and then did, Kennedy pointed to the moon, and then announced to the world when we would be landing!

## Gaining Congressional Support

First, however, Kennedy had to secure congressional approval for this major initiative. His staff began to assess each senator and congressman as a potential supporter or opponent. Their initial rough counts suggested that a majority would support a space program that would aim to put a man on the moon.

After only a few months in office, the new administration had not yet assembled their full arsenal of political tools that could influence the votes of legislators, but they did utilize everything they had. An early, major victory with the space program could have a big impact on establishing the young president as a force to contend with on other issues.

Astutely, Kennedy had assigned the lead role for the space program to Vice President Johnson. Not only was Johnson a well recognized expert and the most vocal space exploration proponent, but perhaps more importantly as former Senate Majority leader, Johnson could round up many of the votes that would eventually be needed to pass the initiative.

Unlike Kennedy, who had a less than stellar career as a senator, and who was not part of the inner circle of the Senate, Johnson was the epitome of a network insider. In 1961, if there was one person who you could choose to be on your legislative team, it would most likely be Lyndon Johnson.

Many historians have credited Kennedy's administrative skills and personnel choices as his strongest asset — not his noted oratory. Assigning Lyndon Johnson the lead role in the space initiative reinforces that assessment. Johnson was somewhat intimidated by the intellectual depth of many of the Kennedy cabinet members; however, he was recognized as a dependable team player that could be counted on to follow the president's directions.

Furthermore, Johnson was a true believer in the space program. On April 20, 1961 at Kennedy's behest, Congress approved an amendment to the Space Act of 1958, which made the vice president, Chairman of the Space Council. In 1960, Eisenhower had tried to abolish it. Yes, the torch had been passed to a new generation of Americans.

Special interest groups can make or break any major legislative attempt. Kennedy had engaged the various departments within the bureaucracy and the scientific community and targeted key senators and congressmen by identifying their states as places to locate some of the new NASA facilities. For example, Overton Brooks (D-Louisiana) who was Chairman of the House Space Committee (1958-1961) was assured that his support would result in a major NASA project in Louisiana — if the proposal was passed.

Likewise, John Stennis, member and former chairman of the Senate Space Committee's authorization subcommittee, was informed that Mississippi needed some space money spent in its state and that the president needed the votes to make it happen. If you can make many of your biggest potential opponents into supporters — before the issue is even announced — your chances of success are greatly enhanced. Kennedy understood this and acted accordingly.

One of the master strokes of Kennedy's strategic approach (my opinion) was that he kept the proposal incredibly simple. In fact, it was not even a piece of legislation. It was merely a proposal to increase the funding of an existing program, with the proviso that the extra funding be allocated to the moon launch and its supporting activities.

There would be no massive or complex documents that would describe in intricate detail each and every step that would be necessary to send a man to the moon. No, Kennedy would only sell an idea and explain why it was imperative that we pursue it. He only sought agreement on the goal — not the details of how to achieve it!

HE ONLY SOUGHT AGREEMENT ON THE GOAL
— NOT THE DETAILS OF HOW TO ACHIEVE IT!

## A TRANSFORMATIONAL APPEAL

On May 25, 1961, President John Kennedy delivered his "Special Message to the Congress on Urgent National Needs." The behind the scenes groundwork had already been laid in place. Every congressional voter who could have been influenced ahead of time had been.

Now it was time to appeal to the remaining congressional voters by using different tactics. By appealing to their patriotism, idealism, and sense of American destiny, Kennedy hoped to use his transformational or motivational style of leadership in a way that could unite the Congress, as well as the American people. Invoking drama and displaying an exquisite sense of timing, he spoke to the Congress, the American people and the world:

> *"I believe that this nation should commit itself to achieving the goal, before this decade is out, of landing a man on the moon and returning him safely to the earth ... But in a very real sense, it will not be one man going to the moon — if we make this judgment affirmatively, it will be an entire nation. For all of us must work to put him there.*
>
> *Let it be clear that I am asking Congress and the country to accept a firm commitment to a new course of action — a course that will last for many years and carry very heavy costs ... If we are to go only half way, or reduce our sights in the face of difficulty, in my judgment it would be better not to go at all.*

*Now this is a choice which this country must make, and I am confident that under the leadership of the Space Committees of the Congress, and the Appropriating Committees, that you will consider the matter carefully ... It is a most important decision that we make as a nation.*

A divided Congress and Senate that had normally been split sharply along party lines came together and gave President Kennedy nearly unanimous support for the manned lunar landing. The Senate voted on June 28, 1961, by a voice vote after very little discussion, and the House followed on July 20, 1961 by a vote of 354 to 59. It was an overwhelming victory by any standard.

Was it luck? Was it a coincidence? Or was it a result of an excellent presidential game plan that included a full range of presidential leadership gambits? JFK and his aides had bartered, cajoled, pressured, and enlisted the help of others to influence many of the congressmen whose support they had garnered during the initial stages of building a base of support. These common methods of transacting the business of politics are usually considered to be the staples of the presidential leadership trade. To that end, the Kennedy administration was more than adept.

However, John Kennedy also had a leadership quality that only some leaders and presidents possess. The ability to speak about important things that are yet to be realized, and in a way makes them seem not only possible, but also in a way that motivates others to want to become part of that realization, is the mark of a special leader.

Winston Churchill, Mahatma Gandhi, Martin Luther King, Jr., and Ronald Reagan, are prime examples of leaders who had this extraordinary quality. John Kennedy was also one of those special leaders.

## A Future Vision and A Grounded Reality

On November 22, 1963, an assassin's bullets ripped through the president as he waved to Americans in Dallas, Texas in the back of an open air sedan. He left us before his first term was finished, but he also left us with a memory of his ideas about a world of possibilities, a world that had a moral compass, and yet a realistic sense of our country's proper place on this planet:

> *"We must face the fact that the United States is neither omnipotent nor omniscient, that we are only 6% of the world's population, that we cannot impose our will upon the other 94% of mankind, that we cannot right every wrong or reverse each adversity, and that therefore there cannot be an American solution to every world problem."* [16]

If Kennedy had lived and been elected to a second term, it is impossible to guess what else he may or may not have accomplished. However, we will always remember what he did accomplish. On July 20, 1969 at 4:18 PM EDT, with only 30 seconds of fuel remaining on the Apollo spacecraft, Neil Armstrong's voice came in over the loud speaker at the NASA control center — "Houston, Tranquility Base here, the Eagle has landed." A thunderous roar erupted in the control center, and it burst the bubble of tension that had gripped the NASA workers who were nervously waiting for the craft to make a successful landing. The NASA controller told the Apollo crew, "You got a bunch of guys about to turn blue, we're breathing again."

... "HOUSTON, TRANQUILITY BASE HERE, THE EAGLE HAS LANDED"

Six hours later at 10:56 PM EDT, Neil Armstrong put his foot on the surface of the moon and spoke those immortal words that would be heard by people on every continent, "That's one small step for a man, one giant leap for mankind." Unfortunately, President Kennedy did not live to hear those words.

However, before Neil Armstrong could take the first step on the moon, someone else had to take the first step toward sending him there. John Kennedy took that first step and he took the rest of us with him. He spoke and we listened. He led and we followed!

... "YOU GOT A BUNCH OF GUYS ABOUT TO TURN BLUE, WE'RE BREATHING AGAIN."

Most presidents (but not all) can handle the routine basics of trading support for one issue in return for the vote on another or employing many other transactional tactics to round up votes.

There is, however, a limit to how much and how often those strategies can be fruitful. Unless a leader can add to those basic leadership talents a higher level of transformational and motivational leadership, he or she will most likely attain only limited achievements. The ability to inspire people to rally around a cause bigger than themselves and to instill a desire in people to dig deeper and strive harder in order to reach new heights is the mark of a special leader.

Leaders must follow through and make sure that their followers are reinforced and re-energized periodically. Sixteen months after securing congressional approval, President Kennedy told a large audience of Americans in Houston's Rice Stadium:

> *"We chose to go to the moon in this decade and do other things in space, not because they are easy, but because they are hard, because that goal will serve to organize and measure the best of our energies and skills, because that challenge is one that we are willing to accept, one we are unwilling to postpone, and one we intend to win ... It is for those reasons that I regard the decision last year to shift our efforts in space from low to high gear as among the most important decisions that will be made during my incumbency in the Office of the Presidency."* [17]

It will always be a matter of conjecture as to what JFK would have ultimately accomplished had he not been assassinated. However, after only six months as president, he had successfully obtained congressional approval for a national agenda that was out of this world.

■  ■  ■

*Man's mind stretched to a new idea never goes back to its original dimensions.*

— OLIVER WENDELL HOLMES

## CHAPTER THREE

# PRESIDENT
# LYNDON B. JOHNSON
# 1963 - 1969
# &
# THE
# GREAT SOCIETY PROGRAM

# ANOTHER
# OPPORTUNITY SEIZED!

*Whatever one may say about the virtues and defects of the War on Poverty and The Great Society, it is clear that Johnson was the greatest presidential legislator in the country's history.*

— ROBERT DALLEK, BOSTON UNIVERSITY

## THE LEGISLATIVE CHAMPION

Unfortunately for many Americans, their memory of President Lyndon Johnson is limited to the travails of Vietnam which dominated the end of his presidency. While criticism of his handling of that ill-fated war is quite widespread, his failure on the international agenda does not negate the incredible successes that he accomplished on the domestic front.

No president, including Franklin Roosevelt, has ever passed as much legislation that so significantly changed our society as did Lyndon Johnson. All presidents bring a unique set of talents, limitations and life experiences to the oval office. Their world view is shaped by everything they have encountered up to the moment they raise their right hand and take the oath.

In 1908, Johnson was born into a hard working family in rural Texas unlike President Kennedy who had come from an extremely wealthy family. Both his father and grandfather had experience as legislators, and so politics was present in Lyndon's life from day one.

After a two year stint as a secretary for a Texas

congressman, in 1935 at age 25, Johnson became the director of President Franklin Roosevelt's National Youth Administration. It was here that some of Johnson's liberal foundation blocks and concepts of the role of the federal government were first put into place.

Starting in 1937, Johnson spent the next twelve years as a democratic congressman, and the following twelve as a democratic senator. In 1951, he became the democratic whip, and in 1953, he was chosen as the party leader. In 1954, when the Democrats took control of Congress, he became the youngest Majority Leader in Senate history. Johnson then proceeded to ignite the formerly sedate Senate into a productive legislative body.

Former Speaker of the House Tip O'Neill worked with both Kennedy and Johnson, and he compared their varied style and approach:

> One reason John Kennedy was so successful as a politician was that he was one of the first to treat politics as a science. Lyndon Johnson was successful in a more traditional way — as a master of the ART of politics. Kennedy was a cool and rational operator who could always tell you exactly what he was doing and why he was doing it; Johnson worked instinctively. Kennedy's political style was in his head, Johnson's was in his blood.[1]

There was also a physical dimension to Johnson's style and tactics. His aura was larger than life. At nearly six feet four inches tall, he usually towered over whomever he was engaging. Big ears, long arms and a prominent nose all seemed to enlarge his personal projection.

The only thing larger than his physical prominence was his personality. Capable of both incredible charm and unbelievably crass and boorish behavior, Lyndon Johnson was truly a force to be reckoned with. No one who interacted with him was left unfazed.

This unique dimension of presidential advantage was obvious to Johnson and he used it as often as possible. In what became commonly referred to as "*The Treatment*," the president would move within inches of an uncommitted legislator. While leaning over his target, Lyndon would invoke whatever tactic he thought appropriate and go to work on the isolated congressman. Two reporters once wrote that it was "an almost hypnotic experience and rendered the target stunned and helpless."[2]

NO ONE WHO INTERACTED WITH HIM WAS LEFT UNFAZED.

Yet "*The Treatment*" was only one of many distinct tools that had a place in the president's legislative tool box. Johnson had a large arsenal of legislative weapons, and he was very skillful with every one of them. Perhaps most importantly, he instinctively knew which tool to utilize or which weapon to employ for a given situation.

*Draw your strength from who you are.*

— RUSSELL MEANS

# THE VICE PRESIDENTIAL YEARS

John Kennedy never started an important meeting unless Vice President Johnson was present. Fortunately, the president was keenly aware that if anything were to ever happen to him, Lyndon Johnson needed to be fully informed on all matters of national interest.

Remembering that President Truman did not know that the United States almost had a deliverable atomic weapon, until after he was sworn into office during World War II, JFK went to great lengths to keep his vice president in the loop.

Despite his insistence that LBJ always be informed of what was actually going on, Kennedy and his closest advisors did not include Johnson in the inner circle of planning and strategy. It was no secret that there was little friendship and even less respect by the Kennedy administration for Lyndon Johnson. Kennedy's Ivy League staff thought that the earthy Texan had served his purpose by delivering his state's electoral votes in the election. Of course, Johnson's eventual role in the Apollo moon launch initiative later proved to be invaluable to the Kennedy administration.

LBJ had never been known to champion the cause of Black Americans during all of his many years in Congress. In fact, he was considered to be more of a conservative than a liberal during his years as a senator. His long political career prior to becoming vice president gave little indication of the monumental liberal legislative initiatives that he would eventually sponsor.

## NOVEMBER 22, 1963

America froze immediately after the bullets ripped into President Kennedy and John Connelly. Stunned by the unexpected and horrific crime and fearful of what it might ultimately mean, our country's citizens were staggered and in a state of shock. Radio reports soon announced that President Kennedy had died, and shortly thereafter, live television showed Lee Harvey Oswald, the alleged assassin being shot and killed by Jack Ruby.

During all of the bizarre events and the surreal atmosphere that had suddenly gripped the nation, Lyndon Johnson was sworn in as president on Air Force One while it carried John Kennedy's slain body from Texas to Washington.

Five days later, President Lyndon Baines Johnson addressed a joint session of Congress and promised to carry on with Kennedy's policies. Reaching out to the Congress and to all Americans, as well as clearing the path for his legislative agenda, he declared:

> *The ideas and the ideals which he so nobly represented must and will be translated into effective action — above all, the dream of equal rights for all Americans.* [3]

He went on to implore the country to highly resolve that John Fitzgerald Kennedy did not live - or die - in vain.

Black Americans and white liberals who had quickly feared that maybe Kennedy's dreams and goals had died with him, were reassured when President Johnson pronounced "no memorial oration or eulogy could more eloquently honor President Kennedy's memory than the earliest passage of the Civil Rights Bill for which he fought so long." [4]

Going on to state the painfully obvious, he pointed out that the country had "talked for one hundred years or more" about equality, and added, "It is time now to write the next chapter, and to write it in the books of law." [5] Johnson utilized every ounce of emotional drama that the assassination had produced and adroitly poured it out as a foundation base upon which he would begin to build *The Great Society.*

## FINISHING KENNEDY'S PRESIDENTIAL TERM

Instinctively being able to recognize an opportunity, and also being able to sense when to capitalize on that opening, is critical for any president. Johnson knew that the dynamics of the country were ripe for leadership. Loss, sympathy, fear, uncertainty and a general sense of a loss of confidence permeated the American landscape in the wake of the Kennedy assassination. The time to act was immediately — and he did!

THE TIME TO ACT WAS IMMEDIATELY — AND HE DID!

Only a few weeks later on January 8, 1964, in his State of the Union Address, Johnson called for a national War on Poverty. The two cornerstones of his grand vision would be racial justice and the elimination of poverty by converting the 23 percent of underprivileged Americans into "tax payers rather than tax eaters."[6] Just two weeks later, the 24th Amendment to the Constitution was adopted. It outlawed poll taxes in federal elections.

... "TAX PAYERS RATHER THAN TAX EATERS"

## HOW DO WE PAY FOR THIS? WE LOWER THE TAX RATE & INCREASE TAX REVENUE!

In order to energize the economy and thus produce more tax revenue to fund his new proposals, the following month LBJ secured passage of Kennedy's tax cut proposal for both personal and corporate taxes. As a result of reducing the tax burden on an overtaxed economy, businesses prospered once again, tax revenues ultimately increased dramatically, and the early phases of *The Great Society* had sufficient tax revenues to sustain them.

BY 1967, AS A RESULT OF THE LARGE TAX RATE REDUCTION, TAX REVENUES HAD INCREASED BY OVER 50 PERCENT.

By 1967, as a result of the large tax rate reduction, tax revenues had increased by over 50 percent. At this point in American history, Congress actually took fiscal responsibility seriously. Johnson knew that unless he could show how he would pay for his new programs, there was a good chance that he might not obtain the necessary congressional votes.

LBJ had immense political skills that were usually utilized behind closed doors and, many times, in one on one encounters. He was not known as a motivational speaker or as a transformational or inspirational leader. However for nearly three years, he quietly watched, learned and assimilated some of these additional leadership traits from John Kennedy.

JFK was charismatic, transformational and a visionary. One of the major aims of this book is to point out the necessity for presidents to learn valuable lessons from their predecessors (both in their successes and failures). Johnson was a perpetual student, and it paid off with handsome rewards.

JOHNSON WAS A PERPETUAL STUDENT, AND IT PAID OFF WITH HANDSOME REWARDS.

Unlike any president before or since, Lyndon Johnson had a broad vision that encompassed the entire landscape of American society. While most presidents focus on a single issue, or merely attempt to put out all of the new brush fires, LBJ was going to attempt to round up many of the country's ills and solve them all in one fell swoop.

## THE GREAT SOCIETY

Exactly six months to the day after the death of President Kennedy, President Johnson made an historic speech at the University of Michigan in Ann Arbor. Some historians feel that this speech marked the beginning of LBJ's campaign for the 1964 democratic nomination. It was here that he began to lay out his grand vision for all to see. Referring to the numerous problems that faced the nation, he foretold of his plans to solve them:

> *We are going to assemble the best thought and broadest knowledge from all over the world to find these answers. I intend to establish working groups to prepare a series of conferences and meetings — on the cities, on natural beauty, on the quality of education, and on other emerging challenges. From these studies, we will begin to set our course toward The Great Society.*

John Kennedy had campaigned in 1960 on the need for our country to compete with the Russians in space. The American people agreed with Kennedy's campaign rhetoric, and the members of Congress knew it.

Johnson also laid out his legislative agenda during the campaign and actively solicited popular support from the American people. This is a critical step in eventually building public pressure that can help to influence the votes of the individual members of Congress after the election.

Some presidential candidates think that just because they have mentioned a particular issue during the campaign, they have set the proper ground work for future legislative attempts. However, unless they have successfully sold a majority of the voters on the merits of that particular issue, they have not laid a solid foundation upon which they can build a legislative strategy.

Johnson understood this fundamental concept, and he used the 1964 presidential campaign to solidify step one of the legislative process. His major focus during the campaign of 1964 was civil rights. He clearly understood the rules of Washington politics, and he used the campaign to properly set the stage for the most productive legislative session in American history. The master was already at work.

As Kennedy's vice president and student, Johnson learned valuable lessons about the use of task forces. JFK had utilized 21 such groups as a specific tactic for preparation for subsequent legislation. Johnson set up 14 task forces, guided by presidential assistants Bill Moyers and Richard Goodwin, to study aspects of American society, and only one of the 14 groups studied international issues.

These groups gave Johnson the dual advantage of putting the major ideas out for general consumption and also allowing much of the early work to be accomplished without the constant scrutiny of the media and the Congress.

LBJ's vision was clearly within our own national borders, yet ironically it was a foreign war that ultimately came to define his presidency. However, in the early stages of his presidency, Johnson's sweeping approach to the entire range of domestic issues was breathtaking and unprecedented.

## THE PRESIDENTIAL ELECTION OF 1964

In 1964, the Republicans committed a blunder that would be copied by the Democrats several times in the years that would follow. In Barry Goldwater, they nominated a candidate from the extreme edge of their party who could not possibly carry enough American voters to win the general election. Mondale, Dukakis and Kerry serve as prime examples of when the Democrats would make the same mistake.

However, the ineptitude of the Republican Party in 1964 greased the skids for Lyndon Johnson's colossal legislative train (*The Great Society*) that would eventually change American culture forever. Legislation establishing equality for all citizens and an incredible explosion of the role of the federal government was about to unfold.

Goldwater's hard line approach to Soviet aggression played into the hands of Johnson's campaign advertisers. The famous television commercial that showed a little girl picking the petals of a daisy, and then being eclipsed by a nuclear explosion, set a new low in "below the belt" campaign tactics. Equating a vote for Goldwater with that of a vote for nuclear war was outrageous and untrue but also effective.

Johnson swept the election with an electoral landslide of 486-52! The Democrats controlled the 89th Congress with a 68-32 margin in the Senate, and 295-140 margin in the House. The new super majorities meant that the congressional rules that had formerly allowed a coalition of Republicans and southern Democrats to stymie many of Kennedy's initiatives were going to be changed. Johnson would be in the driver's seat. He understood the opportunity, but he also knew that opportunities are fleeting. The 89th Congress would be like no other!

THE 89TH CONGRESS WOULD BE LIKE NO OTHER!

## LEGISLATIVE HISTORY — THE 89TH CONGRESS

In 1963 when John Kennedy gave his State of the Union Address, it began with many platitudes such as "this is the side of the hill, not the top." His references to specific things like voting rights were wedged in the middle of a very long speech.

Lyndon Johnson, on the other hand, put the domestic issues at the beginning of the speech. By the fourth sentence, he boldly laid out a challenge, "Let this session of Congress be known as the session which did more for civil rights than the last hundred sessions combined."

As for his legislative agenda, he asked for "the most far reaching tax cut of our time, a war on human poverty, the health needs of our citizens, and reform of our tangled transportation and transit policies."[7]

Shortly after becoming president, Lyndon Johnson lamented "Everything on my desk today was here when I first came to Congress twenty-six years ago."[8] As president during the last leg of Kennedy's term, LBJ had won passage of three of the former president's major proposals in 1964 before he held the office as an elected president — the tax cut, civil rights and antipoverty laws.

... "EVERYTHING ON MY DESK TODAY WAS HERE WHEN I FIRST CAME TO CONGRESS TWENTY SIX YEARS AGO."

With an election mandate that completely legitimized his push for a monumental agenda, LBJ quickly went about dealing with dozens of issues that had been accumulating for decades.

The only major, and perhaps most important, player that was a carry over from the Kennedy administration was Larry O'Brien, the head of the OCR (Organization of Congressional Relations). Much of the Johnson agenda was actually a continuation of the unfinished Truman-Kennedy agenda. O'Brien had not only spent the past three years building an effective machine at OCR, but he had already been actively engaged with many of the proposals that the new president would be promoting.

There would be no need for a learning curve or the requirement of constructing an effective OCR — it was already up and running. The only difference was that Johnson's proposals were much more ambitious than Kennedy's. Kennedy had to deal with the reality of the opposing coalition of southern Democrats and Republicans. — Johnson did not! It would be a new ball game.

Watching a football team that effectively utilizes and manages the last minutes of the fourth quarter is something to admire and appreciate. In sports, in real life, and of course in politics, the clock is always running. Johnson understood that dilemma and made sure that he never wasted a second. In one of his first meetings with his legislative aides after the election, he thundered:

> *I want you to get all of my legislative proposals during this session, now! I lose part of my power. Every day that I use that power, I have less power left ... I want you to get this legislation through now — while I still have that power.*[9]

## THE NEED FOR COMPETENT & TRUSTWORTHY AIDES

LBJ usually reserved *"The Treatment"* for individuals in a private setting. Seven months into his presidency, Johnson began to lose trust in speech writer Richard Goodwin because of suspected leaks to the press. Johnson once remarked, "When Goodwin works on a speech, the press knows it before I deliver it."[10]

The president also began to suspect that his assistant, Bill Moyers, disclosed information for his own benefit. Even though Johnson had always held a special spot for Moyers, he felt that he could not allow anyone to jeopardize the integrity of his agenda. Needing a new assistant, the president brought in Harvard educated Joseph Califano, Jr.

... "WHEN GOODWIN WORKS ON A SPEECH, THE PRESS KNOWS IT BEFORE I DELIVER IT."

Califano described being on the receiving end of *"The Treatment:"*

> *The President called me from Washington to his Texas ranch to discuss the legislative program. Johnson was in the pool when I arrived; he signaled me to join him. We swam for a couple of minutes, then stopped about two-thirds of the way toward the deep end of the pool. At a husky and imposing six feet three, he could stand on the pool floor; at five feet ten I had to tread water because my feet couldn't quite touch the bottom.*
>
> *Poking my shoulder with a strong finger as though punctuating a series of exclamation points, Johnson started talking. He saw America as a nation with many needs: "We'll put together lots of programs and we'll pass them. But there are three big ones I want to be damn sure you*

*do. One, I want to straighten out the transportation mess in this country. We've got to start by getting our own house in order. There are too damn many agencies fiddling with transportation. I want to put them all together in one cabinet department."*

*I nodded, treading. He was so close to me, almost nose to nose, that I couldn't move around him so that I could stand on the bottom of the pool. "Next, I want to rebuild American cities."*

*I was breathing hard.*

*"Third, I want a fair housing bill. We've got to end this Goddamn discrimination against Negroes. Until people"* — *he began jabbing my shoulder as he recited each color* — *"whether they're purple, brown, black, yellow, red, green, or whatever* — *live together, they'll never know they have the same hopes for their children; the same fears, troubles, woes, ambitions. I want a bill that makes it possible for anybody to buy a house anywhere they can afford to. Now, can you do that? Can you do all these things?"*

*"Yes, sir, Mr. President," I responded, not having the faintest idea how. I was electrified by his energy and awed by his ambition even while breathless from treading water as his finger against my shoulder kept pushing me down.*[11]

President Johnson understood the importance of having the right people in the right jobs both behind the scenes as well as in positions of high visibility. Four years earlier, President Kennedy had chosen Johnson to be the lead person for the Apollo space program initiative. Having been the most involved and influential member of Congress on issues involving space, as well as having recently been the former Majority Leader of the Senate, Lyndon Johnson was clearly the most qualified and politically powerful person that Kennedy could have chosen for that role.

As had been the case for President Kennedy, Lyndon Johnson was once again the best person to be the figurehead of the new proposals. The person who is visibly identified as the one who is in charge and leading a proposal can be a great advantage or a major liability.

The passage of Civil Rights legislation was the most important agenda item for President Johnson. Initially, he had assigned the job of spearheading that package of legislation to his Vice President, Hubert Humphrey. Soon, however, Johnson began to feel that Humphrey was not strong enough or shrewd enough to remain entrusted with such an important role.

Joseph Califano adroitly managed to get the vice president to sign a memorandum requesting to be relieved of that duty, even though it was his only substantive assignment. Johnson would take control of that proposal himself.

*If you want a thing done well, do it yourself.*

— Napoleon Bonaparte

## The OCR & Lawrence O'Brien Reach Full Speed

The Organization of Congressional Relations came to life during the Kennedy administration. When President Johnson was ready to unleash the largest legislative initiative in American history (before or since), the OCR had finally hit its stride. Having already defined its role and mission, the president's personal legislative staff had also learned the limits of their capabilities and how to make the most of their small staff and meager resources.

Lawrence O'Brien was the architect of this special unit whose only purpose was to facilitate the passage of presidential proposals. President Johnson knew how effective and valuable O'Brien was, and he set his salary as high as possible at the statutory limit of $30,000!

O'Brien was personally committed to the social agenda that had made little progress under President Kennedy's abbreviated term. He saw Johnson as the person who could actually make it all happen and who was also a fellow true believer. He once remarked about Johnson's leadership style: "I think he saw it as a crusade. It had elements of a crusade, this great battle being waged for right and wrong."[12] The energy and bonding that develops between members of a group that are fighting for a common cause was definitely a factor in their relationship.

If you have ever watched a school of salmon swimming upstream, you surely began to wonder how any of them ever made it to the spawning ground. There are so many obstacles, it seems to be an impossible task.

And so it is with a piece of legislation. A positive action must be taken by a House subcommittee, a House committee, the House Rules committee, the House as a whole, a Senate subcommittee, a Senate committee, the Senate as a whole, and a conference committee. Negative action at any one of these steps can derail a legislative proposal.

Without a special group who can tend to all of the necessary considerations, a president's bill would typically face a very steep uphill battle. That is why Lyndon Johnson relied so heavily upon Lawrence O'Brien and the OCR.

Compared to his predecessor, Johnson's management style was much more hands-on. This resulted in a lot of personal interaction between members of the OCR and the president. This left little room for misunderstanding which was very important because Johnson used the OCR as a filter between himself and individual members of Congress.

If an OCR staffer told a congressman something, it was assumed by all that it accurately reflected the president's thinking on the matter. This even included instances on the floor of the Senate when amendments to a bill were being proposed. If there was a time crunch, the OCR staff member would decide for the administration if the amendment was acceptable or not. They spoke for the president, and he always backed their decision. Johnson insisted that his administration only speak with one voice.

This worked only because Johnson knew that he would always have to support the decisions of the staffers if their credibility was to remain intact. As a result, the OCR earned the respect and trust of many of the formerly suspicious and skeptical members of Congress.

JOHNSON INSISTED THAT HIS ADMINISTRATION ONLY SPEAK WITH ONE VOICE.

Over time, because of Johnson's understanding of the importance of a solid working relationship between his staff and Congress, the OCR became a critical component of the legislative machinery. His insight and the work of O'Brien's staff created a continuous two-way flow of information that became a dependable asset for both the Johnson administration and for the members of Congress.

## TACTICS AND TIMING

The strategy that the OCR used to keep their machine running smoothly consisted of several tactics. Acting as a broker for a mutually beneficial exchange between the administration and a congressman not only facilitated a current issue, it also created a climate that encouraged the congressman to leave that door open for future situations. As a result, that legislator might be more apt to give the president a nod on a close bill that was not critical to his or her district.

On the other hand, O'Brien was very careful not to create a climate of expectations that would result in a congressman always wanting something in return for a vote. It was a delicate balancing act, but they managed it well.

Any good news, such as the administration's support of a congressman's proposed bill, was always delivered by the president or the OCR. Bad news was always delivered by some other source such as the Democratic National Committee or a committee member.

Patronage was a constantly used tool. The availability or unavailability of tickets for tours of the White House, invitations to bill-signing ceremonies, pictures with the president, and invitations to White House social events, birthday calls, invitations to fly on Air Force One and an endless list of other presidential perks could make a difference when it came to assembling votes.

Arm twisting was seldom used, not because Johnson was above such an approach, but because he had learned over the years that it could come back later to hurt him.

Another major tactic was the awarding of project grants. The decisions as to where and when to approve Veterans Hospitals, federal buildings, dams, waterways, military procurements, contracts for local industries and the allocation of the Rivers and Harbors projects of the Army Corps of Engineers all offered the White House opportunities to influence members of Congress.

Nothing is more important to most members of Congress than their own re-election. The awarding of a major project in a congressman's district could make a large impact on the outcome of an election. All parties understood this obvious fact.

This aspect of political control also worked sometimes by maintaining existing projects. Former House Speaker Tip O'Neill told of an early episode that cemented their working relationship. Robert McNamara had recommended that the Boston Naval Yard be shut down. If that happened, it would have had a huge negative impact in O'Neill's district. Tip enacted his own strategy to keep the navy yard open:

> To get the president's attention, I walked out of a meeting of the Rules Committee just before a vote on a bill to reduce federal regulations of rail rates for perishable commodities — a bill the administration cared about. A few days later, Johnson called in the Democratic members of the Rules Committee for one of his periodic meetings. As we were leaving, he took me aside. "Christ," he said, "we had the chance to get that transportation bill out, and you left! What's going on?"

> "Mr. President," I said, "I'm spending a lot of my time trying to save the Boston Navy Yard." "What do you mean?" "McNamara keeps threatening to close it." "Don't you worry about that," said the president. "That navy yard will be around as long as I'm in the White House." [13]

President Johnson understood the need to have the key players like Tip O'Neill on his team. Building a team was one of LBJ's strengths. The OCR was poised to take advantage of these opportunities.

An extremely important relationship developed between the OCR and the leadership of the democratic delegation. Without the support and active involvement of the leadership (both House and Senate), the president's proposals would languish in the never, never land of congressional committees. Johnson and his staff clearly understood this basic concept (not all administrations do).

White House liaisons attended all of the strategy sessions held in the leaders' offices. As time went on, the OCR actually had better information about the potential votes of each legislator than did the Speaker of the House or the Senate Majority Leader.

The realization that the OCR possessed such valuable information created a new dynamic upon which Johnson was able to capitalize. Congressional leaders view the success rate of the legislation that they allow to go to a full congressional vote as a direct reflection of their own leadership abilities. That the OCR had a better accounting of the progress of a bill's potential for actually getting passed put it in a position where the leadership was willing to cooperate with the administration in return for information.

In a nut shell, O'Brien's strategy was to be a valuable resource for individual members of Congress as well as the leadership. Patronage, project grants and a source of vital information became the OCR's stock in trade. They built a highly effective organization that did not even exist six years earlier.

A major consideration that was always part of the ongoing and ever evolving legislative strategy was timing and the intelligent use of time. President Johnson wanted many bills passed as quickly as possible because he knew that his window of political opportunity might end as early as the midterm elections. Actually, he was aware that even as soon as the midterm elections were beginning to take shape that congressmen would only vote for a bill if they thought that it would help their own reelection bid.

Because Johnson was pushing so many different bills simultaneously, consideration had to be given to the best sequence in bringing each bill to a vote. Attempting to influence the speed of each committee, allocating personnel resources to the most important bills and constantly prioritizing schedules was a complicated juggling act. O'Brien's description told of the importance assigned to the time factor:

> *We were very much concerned at all times about the timetable. That was a subject of discussion with the leadership at every meeting. Schedules, schedules, schedules, that took as much time and attention as any other aspect of the process.*[14]

Despite all of the eventual successes, it is hard to overstate the limitations of the staffs. OCR was comprised of less than a dozen staff members. Joseph Califano's staff never exceeded four or five people. That same staff under George W. Bush has exploded to more than one hundred people. The commitment, work output and dedication of Johnson's team are qualities that should make any American proud, regardless of his or her political bias.

JOSEPH CALIFANO'S STAFF NEVER EXCEEDED FOUR OR FIVE PEOPLE. THAT SAME STAFF UNDER GEORGE W. BUSH HAS EXPLODED TO MORE THAN ONE HUNDRED PEOPLE.

## THE USE OF SPECIAL INTEREST GROUPS

Johnson and the OCR constantly attempted to gain any edge that might help them secure votes for various pieces of legislation. Because of limited funding and limited staff, it was important for the group to figure out the best way to maximize its resources.

Soon it was realized that in the same way that the democratic leadership and the OCR could be mutually beneficial, so too could some special interest groups and the OCR if they pooled their resources. This was especially true of organized labor which had a common interest in many pieces of legislation such as education, healthcare, civil rights, and urban development.

The Johnson administration did not have a strong connection with many of the northern legislators, but big labor did. Conversely, big labor was weak in the south and needed legislative assistance with those congressmen on labor legislation, and the administration was in a position to return the favor.

Their opposite strengths provided a marriage of convenience. George Meany, President of the AFL/CIO described why it made sense for them to help each other:

> *You see, he (Johnson) was one President who realized perhaps more than any other President the tremendous influence that organized labor has over on Capital Hill. Now we don't brag about that influence, but it is very definitely there. We of course spend a lot of time and effort in the elections every two years for the Senate and the House, as well as the Presidential election. President Johnson was quite aware of the fact that in some of these liberal measures where a few votes were needed to finally enact the legislation, that our influence in some of these cases could pick up votes that even he couldn't pick up as President; because of our close contact with these members of Congress, and very frankly, because we had helped in a very substantial way in electing them.*[15]

Johnson and Meany met often and spoke to each other on the telephone almost daily. Most of the meetings between the OCR staff and the AFL/CIO took place in the White House. The inclusion of organized labor in such a grand manner created a sense that they were partners with the administration. It was a partnership that Meany would not want to jeopardize, and Johnson knew it. Together, they could each assist each other in obtaining the vote of a congressman that needed to be swayed.

Sometimes there was a three-way approach to legislative cooperation. The democratic leadership, organized labor and the OCR would share information on the potential votes of various legislators and decide which group would be the best to influence the vote of certain members of Congress. This allowed each group to focus its resources on high percentage targets and avoid trying to cover all of the bases. It worked very well for all concerned.

In some cases, however, it was necessary to bring out the big artillery — President Lyndon Baines Johnson. If a vote on an important piece of legislation was going to be very close, the president would call or visit individual members in order to get their vote. He would not do this often because it would lose its effectiveness and perhaps come to be expected. He reserved this tactic for close votes so that only a few legislators would be involved.

At a different level, sometimes the president would have to get a bill out of a committee so that it could actually be put to a vote of the Congress. Wilbur Mills, Chairman of the powerful House Ways and Means Committee, had a bad experience early on when one of the bills that he allowed out of his committee was voted down by a wide margin. After that humiliating defeat, no bill came out of his committee unless he was confident of its successful passage. The relentless Johnson proceeded to personally work overtime to bring Mills on board for his support of the Medicare legislation, one of the president's major bills.

Thinking that he had finally freed the proposal up for a full vote of the Congress, Johnson was angered to find that Harry Byrd, Chairman of the Finance Committee and aligned with the American Medical Association, was bottling up the bill in his committee.

Lyndon Johnson was clever and resourceful, and he never gave up. He was always an active participant in the passage of his own legislation. When Johnson's Medicare legislation was being held hostage by Byrd, he designed a plan to rescue it.

Johnson called Byrd at his farm in Virginia and asked him to come to the White House for a meeting. Byrd thought that it would involve a discussion about an international crisis. After a meeting of the democratic leadership about the Medicare proposal, Johnson led the group that included Byrd into a Cabinet room that was full of reporters and television cameras for a surprise live press conference.

The president went around the table member by member, and he asked each of them to state their position on the proposed Medicare legislation. Every one of them said that it was a good bill and that they intended to vote for it. After perfectly setting up the finale, Johnson turned to Senator Byrd, and the following exchange ensued:

**The President:** *I know that you will take an interest in the orderly scheduling of this matter and giving it a thorough hearing. (Byrd says nothing and stares at Johnson) Would you care to make an observation?*

**Senator Byrd:** *There is no observation I can make now, because the bill hasn't come before the Senate. Naturally, I'm not familiar with it.*

**The President:** *And you have nothing that you know of that would prevent hearings coming about in a reasonable time, not anything ahead of it in the committee?*

**Senator Byrd:** *Nothing in the committee now.*

**The President:** *So when the House acts and it is referred to the Senate Finance Committee you will arrange for the prompt hearings and thorough hearings?*

**Senator Byrd:** *(softly and reluctantly) Yes.*

**The President:** *(banging his hand on the table) Good!* [16]

President Harry Truman had unsuccessfully tried to pass a lesser version of Medicare two decades before. On July 30, 1965, in the presence of Harry Truman in Independence, Missouri, President Johnson signed the Medicare legislation into law.

By using all of his many legislative tools, Lyndon Johnson was able to obtain a high level of bi-partisan support. As Joseph Califano described, "LBJ knew how to persuade men and women by appealing to their noblest — or basest — instincts, or both."[17]

---

*It would be difficult to imagine anyone better equipped for legislative leadership than LBJ.*

— FRED GREENSTEIN

---

However, Johnson also knew how to treat people in a way that was appreciative, respectful and apt to make them want to engage him again in the future. Massachusetts Republican, Silvio Conte, recalled how the president called to thank him "on behalf of the nation for your vote." Conte went on to say that he "damn near collapsed on the spot… It's the only time since I have been in Congress that a President called me."[18]

The largest array of Johnson's leadership arsenal would fall into the category of transactional or the everyday back and forth of barter, compromise, negotiation and trade offs. Like a baseball pitcher who had mastered every kind of pitch, LBJ knew every tactic and had mastered them all.

On the other hand, he was not known for being a transformational or motivational kind of leader. To his credit, however, he would try anything. When it came time for him to begin his quest for the passage of legislation that he believed was morally important, he was willing to step out of his comfort zone and publicly bare his soul. Former House Speaker O'Neill described one such occasion as follows:

> *Johnson's finest hour came on March 15, 1965, when he addressed a joint session of Congress to plead for passage of the Voting Rights Act. It was a spectacular performance, and a great moral statement against discrimination. Nobody who was there, or who saw the speech on television, can ever forget how, in the middle of his remarks, the president raised his arms and announced, "We shall overcome!"* [19]

President Lyndon Johnson held nothing back. He was a man on a mission who was driven by a sense of moral courage that aimed to correct what he saw as injustices of the past and to orchestrate an overhaul of the entire American societal landscape. He intended to finish what Abraham Lincoln had started.

IN 1965, HIS ADMINISTRATION SUBMITTED 87 BILLS TO CONGRESS AND 84 WERE PASSED AND BECAME LAW!

Regardless of whether the reader may agree or disagree with the legislation that LBJ proposed and procured, it is indisputable that Lyndon Johnson was a legislator of epic proportion. In 1965, his administration submitted 87 bills to Congress and 84 were passed and became law!

*The Great Society* bundle of legislation was incredible, not only because of the sheer number of new laws and programs it produced but more importantly because of the scope and range of the issues and problems that it addressed. They included Medicare, Voting Rights, Education, Civil Rights, War on Poverty, Housing, Health, Water Research, Traffic Safety, Minimum Wage, Flammable Fabrics, Economic Opportunity Act, Mass Transit, Highway Beautification, Highway-Safety Act, Model Cities, formation of the Department of Transportation and numerous other significant bills!

Surely one would think that future democratic presidents would have studied this incredible legislative bonanza for lessons that could be learned and put to use in their own administrations. Unfortunately, that would not be the case.

*"It is the excitement of becoming — always becoming, trying, probing, falling, resting, and trying again — but always trying and always gaining ...*
*I used the power of the presidency proudly, and I used every ounce of it I had."*

*— President Lyndon Baines Johnson*

■  ■  ■

---

*I do the very best I know how — the very best I can; and I mean to keep on doing so until the end.*

*— ABRAHAM LINCOLN*

---

# PRESIDENT JIMMY CARTER 1977-1981 & AMERICA'S COMPREHENSIVE NATIONAL ENERGY PLAN

# A MISSED OPPORTUNITY!

■ ■ ■

*It is not enough to have a good mind.*
*The main thing is to use it well.*

— RENE DESCARTES,
FRENCH PHILOSOPHER (1596-1650)

## THE PROBLEM

In November 1976, Americans were still reeling from the Arab oil embargo in 1973, OPEC's (Organization of Petroleum Exporting Countries) price hikes in 1975, Vietnam, Urban Riots, and Watergate. It had been a very tough few years, and the country's confidence was shaken.

Nothing contributed more to the feeling of unease than the realization that foreign countries on the other side of the planet had us in the "proverbial grip," and they were beginning to squeeze.

Americans who took pride in their sense of independence were shocked, angry and somewhat afraid to find that they could be held hostage by a handful of Arab oil ministers. The mood of the country was primed for strong leadership. Americans wanted solutions and they were ready to take action!

BY ALSO CAPTURING THE PRESIDENCY, THE DEMOCRATS WERE NOW IN COMPLETE CONTROL OF THE FEDERAL LEGISLATURE.

In 1976, after eight years of Republican presidents, Americans voted overwhelmingly for

Democrats. The 95th Congress gave the Democrats a huge 61-38 advantage in the Senate, and an even greater edge of 291-144 in the House. By also capturing the presidency, the Democrats were now in complete control of the federal legislature. There was nothing in their way that could possibly prevent them from successfully addressing the country's critical energy challenges — except for Jimmy Carter.

## A BRIEF HISTORY OF PRE-1977 ENERGY POLICY

On October 6, 1973, Jewish people all over Israel were celebrating Yom Kippur, the holy day of atonement. The Sabbath of Sabbaths was disrupted by a massive invasion by Egyptian and Syrian armies. A few months before, King Faisal of Saudi Arabia had warned President Nixon that if America did not support the Arab interests and instead continued to give Israel military and economic aid, there would be serious repercussions. Nixon did not react to the threat. Two weeks later, five Arab ministers and one Iranian met in Kuwait City, and they unilaterally raised the price of a barrel of OPEC oil from $3.00 to over $5.00, a seventy percent increase.[1]

> ... THEY UNILATERALLY RAISED THE PRICE OF A BARREL OF OPEC OIL FROM $3.00 TO OVER $5.00, A SEVENTY PERCENT INCREASE.

97

Despite the developing dynamics of the newly formed oil cartel, Nixon made no adjustments to his budget request for Israel. King Faisal immediately cut off all oil exports to the United States and reduced exports to other countries by 25%. Within days, other Arab countries did the same.

At that time, Americans were at an all-time high for oil wastefulness. Fuel mileage averaged a record low of 13.1 miles per gallon. Over the next three months, the price of a barrel of oil increased more than 400%, from $3.00 to $11.65![2]

Service stations either attempted to ration their supply, or they gouged their customers (some charged over $2.00 a gallon — more than twice the going rate). Policemen were assigned duty at filling stations. U.S. autos sales dropped 11%. General Motors closed 16 plants and laid off 105,000 workers. Chrysler followed suit, closed ten plants and sent 44,000 employees home. Airlines canceled flights, boats stayed in port, and truckers blockaded roads with their rigs.[3]

This crisis seemed to happen all at once. Yet there had been a time when there was too much oil in America. During the Depression, demand was down and huge oil discoveries in east Texas caused an oversupply that caused Congress to create the IOCC (Interstate Oil Compact Commission). It limited oil production for over 35 years in order to prop up the price of oil.

In the 1950's after World War II, an economic boom occurred which significantly increased the demand for oil. However, cheap Venezuelan oil came on the market, and

America was unknowingly on its way to developing an addiction to foreign oil. The Eisenhower administration limited the amounts of cheap oil imports as a way of propping up the price of domestic oil. Conservation was an unknown concept at this point.

The "Perfect Storm" of energy was brewing. While demand was increasing dramatically, future energy supplies were being restricted or eliminated by the environmental movement's strong influence. While many of the environmental concerns were (and still are) valid, it can be argued that a lack of environmental circumspection and sensibility greatly contributed to the energy crisis that threatens America today.

> ... AMERICA WAS UNKNOWINGLY ON ITS WAY TO DEVELOPING AN ADDICTION TO FOREIGN OIL.

## NIXON BEGINS THE ENERGY CRUSADE

In June 1971, Republican President Richard Nixon delivered to Congress the first address in the nation's history that was a plea for action to deal with the growing energy problem, "We cannot take our energy supply for

> ... "WE CANNOT TAKE OUR ENERGY SUPPLY FOR GRANTED ANY LONGER." THE DEMOCRATS YAWNED AND IGNORED HIS REQUESTS.

granted any longer."[4] The Democrats yawned and ignored his requests. The Democrats controlled both the House and the Senate for the entire eight year Nixon/Ford presidency, and they did not offer any alternative comprehensive plan of their own.

By 1973 during the Nixon administration, governmental bureaucracies were multiplying rapidly and contributing to the confusion. Sixty four different federal agencies were created to deal with energy issues. However, they were uncoordinated and many times at cross purposes.

In April 1973 (only a few months before the oil embargo), President Nixon renewed his call for a new cabinet department for energy and natural resources. He said that the issues demanded cabinet level priority and attention.

Nixon also called for multiple plans that would focus on increasing the supply of oil, such as construction of deepwater ports capable of supporting oil supertankers, energy research funds and increased offshore drilling. Once again, the Democrats balked at supporting the president's requests and instead only offered bombastic demagoguery.

Senator Fritz Hollings (D-South Carolina) decried Nixon's plea for multiple strategies of increasing energy supplies as "a step that can only result in billions of dollars of extra cost to the consumers without any assurance that more gas would be committed than is now planned."[5] America's potential energy independence was being sacrificed for the sake of partisan politics.

The Democrats claimed that they wanted an approach that would concentrate on conservation instead of one that would develop new supplies of energy. Why they were not willing to work together in a spirit of bi-partisanship and agree on how to conserve our energy resources while simultaneously increasing supplies, defied common sense, put the Democratic Party's interest ahead of our national interests, and undermined the future security of our country.

Continuing to press the attack for dealing with the growing energy problem, President Nixon used a televised address on November 7, 1973, to tell Americans that "We have an energy crisis" and added that the country was "heading toward the most acute shortages of energy since World War II."[6] Hoping to break the democratic partisan logjam, Nixon reached out and cited the spirit of bi-partisan cooperation that made the Apollo Space Program a national success.

> "WE HAVE AN ENERGY CRISIS"

He called for the formation of ERDA (Energy Research and Development Administration) that would oversee a massive energy research program that would make America energy independent within ten years. He cited the Manhattan project that developed the atomic bomb during World War II as an example of the type of commitment that would be necessary to solve the energy dilemma. The immediate reaction was positive but short lived. Within days, Congress approved the request for the Alaskan pipeline, passed the Emergency Fuel Allocation Act, and lowered the national speed limit to 55 miles per hour.

In January of 1974, a few months after the oil embargo, a Gallup poll found that 46% of Americans thought that the energy crisis was "the most important problem facing the country." Only six months earlier, a similar Gallup poll found that only 4% of Americans considered energy a significant problem.

The American people were beginning to come to terms with reality; however, the crisis temporarily subsided and unfortunately so did the concern of our citizens and the Congress. Energy Czar William Simon declared that "my hardest job ... is to keep the American people awake to the fact that we do have a problem and will continue to have a problem."[7]

> ENERGY CZAR WILLIAM SIMON DECLARED THAT "MY HARDEST JOB ... IS TO KEEP THE AMERICAN PEOPLE AWAKE TO THE FACT THAT WE DO HAVE A PROBLEM AND WILL CONTINUE TO HAVE A PROBLEM."

Seven months later in July of 1974, the Gallup polls showed that only 6% Americans were still concerned about energy. That mood swing popped the balloon of bi-partisan cooperation. Yet while the air of a crisis seemed to have dissipated and the country was lulled back into a sense of complacency, the percentage of imported oil continued to increase. By the end of 1974, imports accounted for 38% of U.S. oil supplies. By 1976, it would be up to 43%!

Later in 1974, the Watergate scandal superseded all other issues. On August 9, 1974, when Gerald Ford became president following Nixon's resignation, the country was able to begin dealing with other national issues, including energy.

Ford, a Republican, believed strongly in capitalism and free trade. He felt that the best way to promote energy conservation was to deregulate the price controls that had been put into place over the past few years. His reasoning was straight out of a high school economics course — if the price of energy increased, consumption would go down. Unfortunately, that concept was a little too difficult for most of the democratic congressmen who controlled the 94th Congress.

The Democrats, who had been claiming to prefer conservation over creating new sources of supply, hypocritically rejected Ford's attempt to conserve oil by allowing its price to be set in a free marketplace. Undeterred, President Ford proposed sweeping energy proposals that caught the Democrats by surprise.

In a spirit of bi-partisan cooperation, Ford offered a compromise solution that included a windfall profits tax on oil companies as a way of placating the obstructionist Democrats, but it was to no avail. The democratic leadership went into a delaying mode and criticized the president's efforts. Senate Majority Leader, Robert C. Byrd (D-West

Virginia) railed against Ford's proposal as a "sock-it-to-the-consumer" scheme.[8]

The Democrats, unwilling to give the Republican president a victory that might be helpful to him in the approaching election, came up with a watered down plan that left the artificial price controls of oil in place. This of course meant that Americans would continue to be sheltered from the reality of true energy costs, and would be less inclined to conserve on energy. Democratic congressional hypocrisy was as thick as a barrel of Arab crude.

DEMOCRATIC CONGRESSIONAL HYPOCRISY WAS AS THICK AS A BARREL OF ARAB CRUDE.

To his credit, President Ford stayed the course. On February 26, 1975, he presented a message on energy and announced sixteen new energy proposals. It included the deregulation of natural gas and declared it "the most important action that can be taken by the Congress to improve our future gas supply situation."[9]

Congress passed only four of the sixteen proposals. Ford did establish the creation of the Strategic Petroleum Reserve to serve as a national emergency backup and compulsory mileage standards for automobiles. However, the energy problem was racing along at about 100 miles an hour while the democratic Congress was still tying its shoes.

## THE 1976 PRESIDENTIAL CAMPAIGN

In the fall of 1976, the year of the country's 200th birthday, campaign rhetoric replaced policy discussions. The democratic nominee, Jimmy Carter, a former peanut farmer and one term governor from Georgia, blasted President Ford for not having secured a comprehensive national energy program: "Almost every other industrialized nation in the world has an energy policy except for us."

Ford shot back and essentially told Carter that he was out of touch and must not have been paying attention for the past two years. President Ford countered that he had attempted on numerous occasions to pass energy bills, but the democratically controlled Congress had prevented their passage and that they were putting our country at risk.[10]

Carter pledged that, if elected president, he would develop a comprehensive national energy plan that would create an energy independent United States. Many Americans were unhappy that President Ford had pardoned Richard Nixon. Despite Carter's lack of national experience and shallow record of accomplishments, many Americans (including this writer) felt that the country needed a fresh start and voted for Jimmy Carter, and he won the election.

The Democrats now had huge majorities in both houses of Congress, as well as control of the office of the presidency. They were in perfect position to demonstrate their leadership abilities and to solve America's critical energy problems. Armed with all of the excellent leadership lessons learned from the last democratic president, Lyndon Johnson, this was an historic opportunity that was as good as it gets for a political party.

## SYMBOLISM OR SUBSTANCE?

In January 1977, the country was in the midst of a bitter cold spell that had produced, for citizens east of the Rockies, the coldest recorded temperatures in the nation's history. Heating oil was being consumed at record levels. After an uninspiring inauguration speech, President Carter and his family walked down Pennsylvania Avenue to the White House. There, they were escorted to a review stand that was being warmed by solar powered heaters where they watched the ensuing parades. The novelty of the solar powered heaters was a precursor to what would be the focal point of Carter's presidency: **energy**.

During the campaign, Jimmy Carter discussed only the need for a comprehensive national energy policy, not what it might look like. As a result, he had not built public support for any specific proposals that he might introduce as president. Additionally, he ran his campaign as an outsider who was critical of the ways of Washington as well as the members of the Washington establishment. Soon, however, he would want their support. Good luck!

## STEP ONE -
## WHO SHOULD LEAD THE PROGRAM?

Jimmy Carter was an engineer by training, and he expected that all problems were solvable if analyzed properly. Since he did not have a deep background in energy matters himself, he looked for an experienced person to head up what was going to be his major legislative agenda — a comprehensive national energy policy. Without giving thought to the full range of political ramifications, Carter chose James A. Schlesinger.

Schlesinger, who had earned a Harvard PhD in economics, was the former head of the Atomic Energy Commission and former director of the Central Intelligence Agency. Despite possessing great credentials, Schlesinger also had a reputation as an arrogant, condescending "know it all" who managed to anger nearly everyone with whom he had contact. Nixon once told an aide "never bring that guy in here again." Responding to criticism of his demeanor, Schlesinger once exclaimed, "God damn it, I am arrogant. I can't stand stupid questions." President Ford fired him as Secretary of Defense.[12]

Omi Walden, the director of the Georgia Department of Natural Resources, urged Carter to appoint someone else

> NIXON ONCE TOLD AN AIDE "NEVER BRING THAT GUY IN HERE AGAIN."

instead of Schlesinger because representatives from many sources such as environmental groups, engineering societies, consumer groups, universities, and even officials from oil producing states all had expressed deep reservations about his proposed role in the administration. The New York Times wrote that he had "a disturbing record on energy issues."[13]

Nine members of the House of Representatives, whose votes would eventually be needed to pass an energy bill, wrote to Carter and argued against his appointment. In what would become classic Carter behavior, he ignored everyone and then decided that Schlesinger was his choice. Carter's front man for energy was extremely intelligent but widely disliked. Not good!

Thomas Sowell's book, *"A Conflict of Visions,"* brilliantly describes the difference between the two predominate philosophies of governing in our society. The first describes a culture that embraces the input and value of all citizens. The other embraces the notion that some members of society are superior, more intelligent, better educated and more informed, and as a result those special individuals should be making the decisions for everyone else. The latter choice of governance clearly applied to the presidential style and attitude of Jimmy Carter.

In keeping with that exclusive philosophy, Carter sent Schlesinger and his staff to secret hideaways where they could go and devise the energy plan. President Carter was considered to be the ultimate micro manager. It was suggested by some that he even managed the schedule for the White House tennis court. Yet inexplicably, he literally turned complete control of his most important agenda item over to a man who seemed to have a perverse pleasure in making people dislike him. Schlesinger also relished the role of keeper of the secret information.

Schlesinger's task force was made up primarily of economists and some administrators who had worked with him in the past. This was the complete opposite of a Lyndon Johnson task force model that included scholars, representatives from the business community, think tanks, trade associations, representatives from the Office of Management and Budget, members of the White House staff, and of course, congressional input. With his elitist mentality, Carter created a task force that was "white, male, and insider oriented. Most were under forty and none had ever worked in any energy related field."[14]

CARTER CREATED A TASK FORCE THAT WAS "WHITE, MALE, AND INSIDER ORIENTED. MOST WERE UNDER FORTY AND NONE HAD EVER WORKED IN ANY ENERGY RELATED FIELD."

## IGNORANCE OR ARROGANCE?

It is hard to imagine that someone who managed to get elected President of the United States could manage to do so many things so badly, and in such a short time, as did Jimmy Carter. Less than a week after the inauguration, Senate Majority Leader, and fellow Democrat, Robert C. Byrd (West Virginia) publicly berated the new president for not including him in the discussions about the energy policy.

An indignant Byrd told the press that the president "has to learn that there have to be a number of senators brought into a discussion on any subject, and he (Carter) better let the leadership know about these meetings so we can suggest the leaders involved."[15] Carter ignored the senator's request. Yet, it was Byrd who would be the most important person that Carter would need in getting an energy bill to clear the Senate. Not a good start!

On the fast track to alienating nearly anyone within range, Carter angered the democratic caucus that controlled both the House and the Senate by ignoring existing congressional protocol, not to mention common courtesy. He saw no need to inform fellow Democrats before appointing people from their state to federal offices. When Carter decided to cut nineteen water projects from a budget bill, the congressmen in the affected districts first learned of the move in their local newspapers.

WHEN CARTER DECIDED TO CUT NINETEEN WATER PROJECTS FROM A BUDGET BILL, THE CONGRESSMEN IN THE AFFECTED DISTRICTS FIRST LEARNED OF THE MOVE IN THEIR LOCAL NEWSPAPERS.

The *Washington Monthly,* a liberal magazine that was not prone to criticize Democrats' shortcomings, recounted a story that involved President Carter's rude and shortsighted behavior with George Meany, the head of the powerful AFL/CIO Labor Union, and a major factor in Carter's election victory.

Carter had lectured Meany on why he should promote wage concessions as a way to help fight inflation. After the president had issued his directive, he began to head for the door. Meany spoke up and said, "Wait a minute, Mr. President. I want you to hear our response." Carter listened to Meany make a case why it would not be a good thing for American workers to have to bear the brunt of the fight on inflation. Carter stood up and retorted, "If you can't support me I'd rather not talk" and then he left in a huff.[16] Of course, George Meany was now much less motivated to help Carter round up votes for future issues. Did Jimmy Carter ever consider the long-term implications of his own behavior?

> "IF YOU CAN'T SUPPORT ME I'D RATHER NOT TALK"

## NOT READY FOR PRIME TIME

It became obvious to even a casual observer that Jimmy Carter was in way over his head and that he was probably one of the few remaining people that did not know it.

Joseph Califano, an experienced Washington insider who agreed to be in Carter's administration, described his initial interactions with Carter and his staff members:

> With my background in government, I was prepared for monumental policy disputes over welfare reform and national health insurance. But I was not prepared for the way in which President Carter tried to negotiate the political rapids of the disputes that arose over these issues. From the first meeting of his cabinet at Sea Island, Georgia, over the Christmas holidays in 1976, I had sensed a naiveté among the President and his key staffers about the Washington world.[17]

House Speaker Tip O'Neill's reaction mirrored Califano's:

> When it came to the politics of Washington, D.C., he (Carter) never really understood how the system worked. And although this was out of character for Jimmy Carter, he didn't want to learn about it either.[18]

After the election but before the inauguration, O'Neill and Carter met to discuss the future. The Speaker informed the new president how important it would be that he work along with Congress in order to get his agenda approved. Carter proceeded to inform O'Neill that when he was governor and ran into legislative resistance, he simply went over the heads of the legislators and made a direct appeal to the voters. Incredulous, the Speaker raised his voice and bellowed, "Hell, Mr. President, you are making a big mistake. You don't mean to tell me that you're comparing the House and Senate with the Georgia legislature? The Congress of the United States includes some of the most talented and knowledgeable lawmakers in the world."[19] Unfortunately, O'Neill was wasting his breath.

Powerful congressman Dan Rostenkowski (D-Illinois), who was also disappointed at the lack of respect and aloofness of President Carter and his staff, responded to press inquiries about the status of the proposed energy policy, "I don't see this Congress rolling over and playing dead." Issuing a warning to the president, Rostenkowski added, "Carter is going to set up his priorities and we are going to set up ours. We'll see where we go from there."[20] Jimmy was not in Georgia any more!

It is hard to understand how a President of the United States did not understand that members of Congress had some of the largest egos on the planet. Whether he liked it or not, those congressmen would make or break his presidency. Obviously (you would think), he and his staff

"HELL, MR. PRESIDENT, YOU ARE MAKING A BIG MISTAKE. YOU DON'T MEAN TO TELL ME THAT YOU'RE COMPARING THE HOUSE AND SENATE WITH THE GEORGIA LEGISLATURE?"

would need to be aware that these valuable players should be recognized and treated as VIPs.

Democratic whip, John Brademas, was not amused that every time he called the White House, he had to spell his name for the receptionist. His indignation was ignored by Carter's staff, and now one more congressman was left wondering what was meant by the phrase "southern charm and hospitality."

Not surprisingly, it wasn't only the president's fellow Democrats who were frustrated by Carter's lack of political experience and lack of a spirit of cooperation. House Minority Leader, John Rhodes (R-Arizona), publicly criticized the administration for "a complete lack of understanding of how the Congress works and the proper relationship between the Congress and the White House."[21]

## CARTER'S STAFF FOLLOWS IN HIS FOOTSTEPS

Joseph Califano was perhaps the most able, politically astute and experienced member of the Carter administration. It is surprising that he was asked to serve because he was so completely out of place in Carter's inner circle of Georgia confidants. His reflections describe the abrupt change in the political environment, "For all my Washington experience, I was not prepared for the cultural chasm between me and President Carter and his closest Oval Office aides."[22]

Tip O'Neill described his impression in a similar fashion: "Too many of Carter's people — especially Hamilton Jordan, the President's top aide — came to Washington with a chip on their shoulder and never changed."[23]

Probably the two most important people that would impact the success or failure of President Carter's legislative agenda were Senate Majority Leader, Robert Byrd, and House Speaker, Tip O'Neill.

"FOR ALL MY WASHINGTON EXPERIENCE, I WAS NOT PREPARED FOR THE CULTURAL CHASM BETWEEN ME AND PRESIDENT CARTER AND HIS CLOSEST OVAL OFFICE AIDES."

Each of them would (or would not) make critical decisions about how a particular bill would be guided through their respective legislative chambers. Common sense would dictate that a special relationship should be cultivated with these key players. However, even before Carter was sworn in as president, his staff was poisoning the well.

There was a White House party the night before the inauguration. Each congressman was allowed to purchase seats for guests at $25 a ticket. The new House Speaker bought a dozen seats for his family. During the affair, O'Neill kept looking for his family but could never see them. He later found out why. His family was assigned the worst seats in the house in the last row of the second balcony.

O'Neill called Hamilton Jordan the next day and said,

> *Listen you son of a bitch. When a guy is Speaker of the House and his family gets the worst seats in the room, he figures there's a reason behind it. I have to believe that you did that deliberately.*

Sarcastically, Jordan answered,

> *If that's the way you feel about it we'll give you back your three hundred bucks.*

Angered, O'Neill shot back,

> *Don't be a wise guy. I'll ream your ass before I'm through.*[24]

Obviously, Hamilton Jordan never read Dale Carnegie's book, *How to Win Friends and Influence People*. After less than a week on the job as president, Jimmy Carter had managed to get Senator Byrd to publicly denounce him and his new administration, and Speaker O'Neill to threaten to get even with his top aide. This was not a high point in the history of legislative strategy for the Democratic Party.

Unfortunately, things would not improve. Jordan, Carter's top advisor, was perhaps even more clueless than arrogant. He never attended any of the White House breakfast meetings where upcoming legislation was discussed. In the four years of the Carter administration, Jordan only met with the Speaker of the House three times. Maybe that is why O'Neill referred to Hamilton Jordan as "Hannibal Jerkin."[25]

A person could find the endless list of faux pas, miscues, and needless blunders of Jimmy Carter and his buddies from Georgia to be humorous, amusing and perhaps even entertaining. However, Carter and his clueless cast of characters were holding the future of America's energy security in their hands, and they were playing with it like a pistol that they did not know was loaded.

MAYBE THAT IS WHY O'NEILL REFERRED TO HAMILTON JORDAN AS "HANNIBAL JERKIN."

## KISS (KEEP IT SIMPLE STUPID)

After three months of secret meetings, Schlesinger and his team came back to the president with an incredibly complex plan that was virtually incomprehensible to an ordinary human being, much less a congressman.

In an attempt to camouflage the main thrust — deregulation of oil which would allow the price to increase and thus promote conservation — Schlesinger created multiple formulas and several series of complex calculations that would ultimately determine the price of oil and gas.

Despite the complicated and convoluted calculations that were concocted by Schlesinger and his staff (which only an engineer or a mathematician could understand), they some how forgot to account for any analysis of how the plan might impact the U.S. economy.

Secretary of the Treasury, Michael Blumenthal, and Economic Advisor, Charles Schultze, both told Carter that without an accompanying analysis that showed that the energy proposal was economically feasible, the chances of securing passage were remote at best. They went on to add that the policy team needed to be expanded which was a subtle way of reminding Carter that

> "SCHULTZE AND BLUMENTHAL TREAT ME LIKE I'M AN IDIOT."

they were still angry at being excluded from Schlesinger's "invitation only" inner circle.

Jimmy Carter did not take criticism well, and he complained to assistants Hamilton Jordan and Frank Moore that "Schultze and Blumenthal treat me like I'm an idiot."[26] Yet the reality was that the entire proposal was incomplete, not well thought out and in danger of unraveling before it was even presented to Congress. Carter and his staff scurried to regroup so that they could deliver an energy proposal to Congress by the self-imposed deadline of "within the first 90 days."

Ninety-one days into his presidency, Jimmy Carter addressed a joint-session of Congress to introduce his comprehensive energy plan. He implored the nation and the Congress "to act now — together — to devise and to implement a comprehensive national energy plan to cope with a crisis that could otherwise overwhelm us."[27]

His proposal was soup to nuts, A to Z, and it included alternative energy research, ethanol use (known then as gasohol), gas guzzler taxes, and numerous other proposals. The over-arching theme however was conservation (increasing the price of oil) not an attempt to increase oil supplies. There were a staggering 113 separate proposals in all.

To his credit, Jimmy Carter looked into the future, saw the energy crisis approaching and tried to adjust America's course accordingly. His predecessor, Gerald Ford had seen the same future, and he, too, had made several valiant attempts to secure our nation's energy independence.

> THERE WERE A STAGGERING 113 SEPARATE PROPOSALS IN ALL.

Unfortunately, a Congress that was strongly controlled by large majorities of Democrats in both the House and Senate, many of whom were the hired guns of special interest groups like big labor and the auto industry, defeated the majority of Ford's initiatives. They were about to do the same to Jimmy Carter's.

## STEP TWO - HOW CAN WE GET THIS THING PASSED?

Immediately after his address to Congress, Carter realized that the American people were not solidly in his camp. During his campaign, he had not properly cultivated public support for any specific energy goals, much less specific plans for action. He and his staff had already alienated many members of Congress, the media, and special interest groups. Most importantly, he and his staff had managed to anger both the Speaker of the House and the Senate Majority Leader.

Nearly everyone who had a stake in the upcoming legislative proceedings had been excluded from the initial planning stages, and as a result, they were all suspicious and many were now less than neutral. If that was not bad enough, the energy plan was extremely complex, and the 113 separate proposals, were enough to make even the most astute congressman's eyes glaze over.

It appeared that Carter and his administration had bungled the opportunity so badly that there was really little hope of passing a comprehensive energy plan so critical for the future security of the United States. However, in America there is always hope — not always a guarantee of success — but always hope and possibility.

Many Americans (including this writer) disagreed with many of the extremely liberal agendas that Tip O'Neill supported and worked to establish over his long and distinguished congressional career. However after extensive research, I have come to consider him a true American hero and a congressman that in some very important ways should serve as an example for elected officials today.

After being on the receiving end of Jimmy Carter and his cronies' rude, disrespectful, and condescending behavior, it would not have been a surprise if O'Neill had simply let Carter's energy plan go down in flames and even taken some pleasure in watching his tormentors twist in the wind.

The heart and soul of Carter's energy proposal was to lift oil price regulations, and let prices rise in order to force public conservation. The Democratic Party (O'Neill's party), aligned with many of the special interest groups in Detroit, was against that approach. The Speaker had no vested interest whatsoever in supporting the legislation except that he thought that it was in the best interest of the country.

Rising above the personal slights and professional disrespect, Tip O'Neill went on a mission to secure passage of the energy bill. Importantly, he understood that the scope of the proposal was so broad that it could potentially be broken up into many little pieces and sent to various committees and subcommittees. If that happened, the bill would be torn apart, chopped up, have dozens of additional provisions added, and if it actually made it through the House of Representatives, it would bear no resemblance to the original bill.

> THE SPEAKER HAD NO VESTED INTEREST WHATSOEVER IN SUPPORTING THE LEGISLATION EXCEPT THAT HE THOUGHT THAT IT WAS IN THE BEST INTEREST OF THE COUNTRY.

O'Neill told the president that he would devise a plan that would allow him to keep the proposal all in one piece, and as a result, it would be voted on by a strictly yea or nay basis. The Speaker felt that an all or nothing approach would afford the greatest chance of success. He was right!

O'Neill's adroit handling of the technicalities and the procedural issues did result in a successful vote in the House. Miraculously, the proposal was now half way to enactment. Only Senate approval stood in the way of the passage of a comprehensive energy plan that, while not perfect, could have taken a giant step forward toward making the United States energy independent.

## ROBERT BYRD WAS NO TIP O'NEILL

In 1958, Robert Byrd, a former small-town food store operator from West Virginia, was elected to the U.S. Senate. Unassumingly, he worked his way up the ranks of the democratic leadership. Unexpectedly in 1971, he out maneuvered Ted Kennedy for the Majority whip. Six years later, Byrd won the Majority Leader's post after a hard fought battle against Hubert Humphrey.

He was unusually stiff and formal when he made a public address. Lacking charm and charisma, Byrd's limited leadership abilities concerned many of his colleagues, and they did not support him in his run for the Majority Leader's job. When asked about his shallow leadership skills, he would often respond with Popeye's famous line "I yam what I yam and that's all I yam."[28] The opportunity to secure an energy independent America was now potentially resting on the shoulders of one man — Senator Robert Byrd.

The Senate Majority Leader was quick to inform listeners that he did not intend to become "the President's point man." Soon he announced that he would not be setting up a special committee in order to keep the proposal in one piece, nor would he shepherd the bill through the upper house. Unlike O'Neill, who had created a special committee to keep the proposal intact and put the bill on the fast track in order to increase its chance for passage, Byrd's approach to the energy legislation was one of benign neglect.

Again unlike Speaker O'Neill, Majority Leader Byrd did not develop a strategy for securing passage of the bill. He did not even set a timetable for energy hearings. His response to critics about his lackadaisical approach as Majority Leader on such an important bill was, "let the Senate work its will."[29]

Byrd then proceeded to split the bill into six pieces and send them to various committees. This meant that the bill would lose any cohesion and would not

> ... BYRD'S APPROACH TO THE ENERGY LEGISLATION WAS ONE OF BENIGN NEGLECT.

be voted on as a coordinated and interrelated set of strategies that together could effectively deal with energy.

This opened the door for the special interest groups and lobbyists to swoop down on the isolated pieces of the proposal. As a result, many parts of the bill were gutted, amended, or weakened. Additionally, infighting within the Senate itself soon exposed other difficulties that would confront the bill.

Henry "Scoop" Jackson (D-Washington) was Chairman of the Energy Committee. He was considered by many of his colleagues to be the resident expert on energy matters, and he had resisted all prior efforts to end the artificial price controls on the oil industry. Russell Long (D-Louisiana) was Chairman of the Finance Committee. He had always been an ardent supporter of efforts to end price controls. Long argued that Carter's plan did too little to encourage new production of oil, and Jackson argued that Carter's plan would subject Americans to the real price of oil and that he was opposed to such a radical idea. Reality was definitely off limits and would not be part of the democratic agenda.

Like vultures on road kill, the Senate picked away at the numerous provisions of the bill. The Energy Committee gutted the request for utility rate reform and neutered the coal conversion bill. The Finance Committee rejected the gas guzzler tax and then rejected the centerpiece of the energy plan, the crude oil equalization tax.

LIKE VULTURES ON ROAD KILL, THE SENATE PICKED AWAY AT THE NUMEROUS PROVISIONS OF THE BILL.

After the blood began to spurt and the feathers began to fly, Senator Abraham Ribicoff, (D-Connecticut) publicly mused, "I'm just wondering … if the President shouldn't admit that his energy program is in a shambles."[30]

On September 24, 1977, the headline that appeared in the <u>Congressional Quarterly Weekly</u> told the story well: **"Senate Hacks Up Carter Energy Program."**

## CARTER REFUSES TO COMPROMISE

By October of 1977, the Senate had finished ravaging the proposal and sent their new version to a conference in an attempt to reconcile it with the House version which was essentially Carter's initial proposal. Not surprisingly, a deadlock ensued. Once again, Carter was tone deaf to the ways of Washington and refused to compromise in any way. For example, the United Auto Workers (UAW) demanded that requirements for the production of fuel-efficient automobiles be eliminated. Instead of negotiating for less stringent requirements and perhaps actually securing some concession from big labor, Carter, as usual, stayed with his "my way or the highway" position. Big labor said "No Way!"

Unlike the House that passed a bill in only a few months, the joint conference stumbled along for nearly two years until May 1978. The significantly modified congressional compromise that passed was only a shadow of the original proposal.

Timing is always a major factor in any negotiation. Now the midterm elections were approaching, and any merits that the bill might contain took a distant second seat for consideration for any congressman who was up for re-election. "Will voting for this bill help **ME** or hurt my reelection chances?" became the driving question that guided its destiny.

Only Robert Byrd knows for sure why he chose to throw the proposed energy program like a hunk of meat into the Senate shark pool. Perhaps he did not really care about energy as an issue and failed to understand the real importance of addressing the energy crisis at that time. Maybe he was so angry at Jimmy Carter and his staff for their lack of respect for him and the Senate as an institution that he was not about to help them pass their legislation. Some people have surmised that Robert Byrd simply did not have the political horsepower to lead the Senate the way that Tip O'Neill was able to lead the House of Representatives.

Senator Byrd has continued to be a U.S. Senator to this day. He has become the unofficial King of Pork Barrel spenders. There are probably more federal buildings in West Virginia that are named after Robert Byrd than there are in any other state for any other senator. He has become a walking, talking one man advertisement for the absolute need for congressional term limits.

However in early 1977 when Robert Byrd was staring into the face of both a crisis and an opportunity, unfortunately for America, he blinked. Perhaps today he relates to the famous movie line from "On The Waterfront" that Marlon Brando made famous, "I coulda been somebody!"

## CARTER - THE PATRIOT

On November 9, 1978, President Jimmy Carter signed the National Energy Plan into law. It was, however, a shallow victory. More symbolic than substantive, the new legislation was not nearly enough to realistically deal with America's growing energy problem. Lesser men would have called it a day, counted it as a win and moved on to some easier legislative target.

While Jimmy Carter was short on leadership skills and like a duck out of water in the big pond of Washington politics, he was also a man of character, perseverance, and determination. A true American patriot, Carter climbed back into the ring and continued to take a political pounding because he believed that fighting for a realistic energy program was the right thing to do. Bloodied, bruised and exhausted, he got off the stool and came out for another round.

> BLOODIED, BRUISED AND EXHAUSTED, HE GOT OFF THE STOOL AND CAME OUT FOR ANOTHER ROUND.

To his credit, Carter's leadership style had been tempered by his initial losses, and he and his staff began to develop a more inclusive approach. Schlesinger was eventually removed, and Carter's staff adopted a more professional tenor. It would be too little, too late.

## OUTSIDE FACTORS OVERPOWER THE AGENDA

Unfortunately, world events and economic turmoil became major factors that seriously undermined Carter's second attempt at passing a comprehensive energy bill. Inflation was approaching 20%, unemployment was rising dramatically, and interest rates on home loans were nearly 18%. The new way of keeping score on the economy was now calculated as the "misery index." Ironically, while Carter was desperately attempting to deal with America's growing dependence on Arab oil, major events in the mid-east would help to undermine his efforts.

In 1953 during the Eisenhower administration, Mohammed Reze Pahlavi (The Shah of Iran) reclaimed his throne in Iran with the help of a CIA-backed coup. He instituted a huge military buildup using the large and steady stream of oil money that came in from western countries like the United States.

THE NEW WAY OF KEEPING SCORE ON THE ECONOMY WAS NOW CALCULATED AS THE "MISERY INDEX."

Like many Arab rulers, he used brutality to subjugate the Iranian citizens. The Muslim community was angered at America for having helped the Shah regain power. Additionally, the Islamic fundamentalists did not want elements of western culture to infiltrate their countries. They strongly resented foreign cultural influences that they

*Whatever you wish that men would do to you, do so to them;*
*for this is the law and the prophets.*

— JESUS (A.D. 1ST CENTURY). MATTHEW 7:12

felt were negatively affecting the behavior and thinking of the Iranian people.

The Islamist militants attributed the culture creep primarily to America's involvement with the Shah of Iran and the long standing relationship between the U.S. and Saudi Arabia. President Franklin Roosevelt first cut a deal with the Saudis after World War II. In exchange for U.S. protection from hostile Arab neighbors, the Saudi Royal Family would provide a steady supply of oil.

At that time, America did not even need Saudi oil. FDR made this arrangement in order to guarantee that our European allies would have a dependable supply of oil while they rebuilt their continent after the war. The fear was that the Soviet Union would take control of mid-east oil if we did not beat them to it.

Without exception, every American president since Franklin Roosevelt has stayed with the same policy of keeping American military, American personnel, and thus the presence of American culture, in Muslim countries

*Actions will be judged according to intentions.*

— MUHAMMAD, THE SAYINGS OF MUHAMMAD, 1, TR.
ABDULLAH AL-SUHRAWARDY, 1941

that find much of our culture reprehensible by their own standards. If the tables were reversed and another country imposed itself in a similar manner in the United States, Americans would be outraged — and rightfully so! It is in that context that we must analyze the events that followed.

> IF THE TABLES WERE REVERSED AND ANOTHER COUNTRY IMPOSED ITSELF IN A SIMILAR MANNER IN THE UNITED STATES, AMERICANS WOULD BE OUTRAGED — AND RIGHTFULLY SO!

It should have been no surprise that Iranian support for a militant like the Ayatollah Khomeini, who advocated the overthrow of the Shah and a cleansing of the "evil" western culture from their country, took hold. The Shah was deposed and sent into exile.

The Iranians embraced a cultural revolution that harkened back to a fundamentalist value system of a prior era. While many Americans found (and still do) the Iranian mentality to be incomprehensible, it is important to remember two things. First, Iran is their country — not ours. Second, they feel the same way about us, and they want us and our culture to

> FIRST, IRAN IS THEIR COUNTRY — NOT OURS. SECOND, THEY FEEL THE SAME WAY ABOUT US, AND THEY WANT US AND OUR CULTURE TO VACATE THEIR REGION.

vacate their region.

The Shah became seriously ill while in exile and requested permission to come to the United States for treatment. The Carter administration approved the request, and as a result, angered the militant Muslims who detested the deposed "evil American puppet" (the Shah).

On November 4, 1979, at about 3:33 am EST, Elizabeth Ann Swift, the political officer at the U.S. embassy in Teheran, placed an emergency call to the State Department. She said that angry demonstrators had broken down the gates and had surrounded the building. An hour or so later, she called again and in a panic said that the demonstrators had stormed the building and were tying up embassy personnel. She screamed, "We're going down! We're going down!" Then the phone went silent.

> SHE SCREAMED, "WE'RE GOING DOWN! WE'RE GOING DOWN!" THEN THE PHONE WENT SILENT.

Soon blindfolded American captives were paraded on international TV as a way of embarrassing the United States. Their captivity would dominate the events of the remaining 444 days of the Carter presidency. A few weeks later, the Soviet Union invaded Afghanistan. The quest for an energy plan was quickly moving to the back burner.

## COURAGEOUS BUT CLUELESS

The energy goals were still on Carter's radar screen. Despite continual setbacks, President Carter continued to make a case for the need of a national energy plan. Unfortunately, as president he was lost, had no map, refused to ask for directions and probably did not even realize that he was lost. After another of his many addresses to the nation, the president and House Speaker O'Neill had the following exchange:

> O'Neill: *That was a fine address Mr. President. Now here is a list of members you should call to keep the pressure on, because we will need their votes.*

> Carter: *No, I described the problem to the American people in a rational way. I'm sure they'll realize that I'm right.*

> O'Neill: *Look, this is politics we're talking about here, not physics. We need you to push this bill through.*

> Carter: *It's not politics, not to me. It's simply the right thing, the rational thing. It's what needs to be done.*[31]

Why Jimmy Carter did not realize that part of his job was to facilitate the passage of his own legislative agenda is almost too bizarre a question to contemplate. Had he never heard of Lyndon Johnson, or ever wondered why the last democratic president before him was so successful and why he was having such a difficult time himself? Learning lessons from the successes and failures of former presidents was not part of Carter's action plan.

... "ONE OF THE WORST DAYS OF MY DIPLOMATIC LIFE."

On the world stage over thirty years ago, other industrialized countries had seriously begun to address energy issues, and they expected the U.S. to do its part as well. President Carter went to an international conference in Tokyo where energy discussions dominated the agenda. The Europeans and Japanese acrimoniously lambasted him for America's failure to reduce its energy consumption. Later that night, he wrote in his diary that the session had been "one of the worst days of my diplomatic life."[32]

Back in America, Detroit's special interest groups had their congressional puppets essentially dancing on strings to the tune of "If you want to get re-elected, you better do as we say." The best interests and future security of America were being sold out to the automobile manufacturers and labor unions.

Even many Democrats (but not enough) were outraged at the shameless prostitution. Richard Bolling (D-Missouri) bitterly complained, "This is the most gutless Congress I've ever served in, and I served during the McCarthy years."[33]

The once proud Democratic Party, which just a few years earlier under its last president had accomplished more progressive social legislation than at any other time in American history, was now reduced to a group of obstinate obstructionists.

> "THIS IS THE MOST GUTLESS CONGRESS I'VE EVER SERVED IN, AND I SERVED DURING THE MCCARTHY YEARS."

Confused by his inability to find support for his energy program, on July 15, 1979, Jimmy Carter once again addressed the nation. He essentially blamed the American people for the country's woes, citing a "crisis of confidence … that strikes at the very heart and soul and spirit of our national will."[34]

He may have been correct in his assessment. However, given that there had been poor leadership coming out of Washington for the prior three years, it would have been understandable if the American people were feeling a bit uneasy.

Just as the first energy bill had been decimated and passed pretty much in name only, Carter's second energy bill suffered the same fate. On June 30, 1980, he signed the Energy Security Act. That was Jimmy Carter's last effort to move America toward a position of energy independence.

As an American, I am proud of him for tenaciously pushing forward for the entire four years of his presidency. As he said in February 2007, "I spent more time on the energy issue while I was president than any other thing I addressed."[35]  Jimmy Carter's relentless drive, despite ever increasing obstacles, demonstrated an important presidential trait that would make any American proud.

On the other hand, many Americans (including this writer) were frustrated, disappointed, and angry that he was so hard headed, self righteous, and so unwilling to utilize any leadership skills.  His refusal to take advice or study the lessons learned from former presidents was simply inexcusable.  America's golden opportunity to become a nation that could control its own energy destiny slipped through his fingers.

However, he was not the only participant that deserves blame. A majority of the democratic congressmen in the 95th and 96th Congress tarnished the good name of the Democratic Party, and they sold out our country to special interest groups. Thomas Friedman, a renowned columnist for the New York Times, wrote an article in January 2007 in tribute to President Gerald Ford's initial role in the quest for a national energy plan.  Referring to the

> "I SPENT MORE TIME ON THE ENERGY ISSUE WHILE I WAS PRESIDENT THAN ANY OTHER THING I ADDRESSED"

---

*Some men change their party for the sake of their principles, others their principles for the sake of their party.*

— ANONYMOUS

---

miles per gallon requirements that were first instituted by Ford, Friedman wrote:

> *Those mileage standards have barely been tightened since 1975 — because some idiotic congressmen from Michigan, who thought they were protecting Detroit, have blocked efforts to raise them. So, Japanese automakers innovated more in that area, and the rest is history — or in the case of Detroit, obituary."* [36]

America's space agency, NASA, recently had a group of its engineers test drive a fleet of German made BMW "Hydrogen 7" fuel cell test cars. These hybrids run pollution-free on a renewable source of fuel. At the same time, Detroit introduced a new fleet of "retro muscle cars" that crank out over 400 horse power, and average about 12 miles per gallon. What is wrong with that picture?

President Gerald Ford lit the torch of energy independence and ran with it as hard and as long as he could. He passed the torch to President Carter, who got lost along the way, but who kept running for four years. He passed the torch to Ronald Reagan who dropped it. George H.W. Bush, Bill Clinton, and George W. Bush all looked at the torch lying on the ground — but never picked it up. The torch is still burning but still lying on the ground. Would someone **PLEASE** pick it up, and start running — quickly!

■  ■  ■

## CHAPTER FIVE

PRESIDENT
BILL CLINTON
1993 - 2001
&
AMERICA'S
COMPREHENSIVE
NATIONAL
HEALTHCARE PLAN

ANOTHER
MISSED OPPORTUNITY!

■ ■ ■

*Talent alone won't make you a success.*
*Neither will being in the right place*
*at the right time — unless you are ready.*
*The most important question is:*
*"Are you ready?"*

— JOHNNY CARSON

## THE PROBLEM

If you have ever driven a car in England, Scotland or Ireland you quickly realize that everyone else is driving on the "wrong" side of the road. You must quickly make a choice. Either you continue to be "correct" and probably end up getting killed, or you adjust accordingly and go with the flow. And so it is with healthcare. I believe that more American jobs are lost to foreign workers because of healthcare costs than any other single reason. That is because companies in other countries do not have healthcare costs.

I BELIEVE THAT MORE AMERICAN JOBS ARE LOST TO FOREIGN WORKERS BECAUSE OF HEALTHCARE COSTS THAN ANY OTHER SINGLE REASON.

For example, when Detroit must add up all of its costs in order to properly price a car, it must include approximately two thousand dollars extra (and counting) for healthcare for both workers and retirees. In Japan and Germany, Toyota and Mercedes, as well as other foreign competitors, do not have that expense because their healthcare is being provided at the national level. As a result of the price difference, fewer Detroit made cars are being purchased, and so fewer American autoworkers are needed — but Toyota is hiring. This is not complicated.

General Motors currently pays healthcare costs for three non-producing retirees, for every one working employee (270,000 retirees and 73,000 workers). GM's $50,000,000,000 healthcare liability could very easily bankrupt the pathetically weak automobile manufacturer. Ford is in a similar predicament.[1]

## THE OTHER PROBLEM

When the U.S. dollar regains strength, it could be the final nail in the coffin for the U.S. automobile industry. The weak dollar requires Americans to pay significantly more for imported cars and trucks because it takes more dollars to convert to the foreign currency. In January 2004, only $.79 (U.S.) was necessary to purchase a product that was priced at one Euro. In June 2008, because of the recent sharp decline in the value of a dollar, that same product would now cost $1.56 (U.S.) – nearly double!

While not visible to the consumer, the currency conversion to dollars is necessary to price any imported product - including automobiles. It is now much more expensive to purchase a Mercedes, BMW, or Volvo than it was just four years ago. This currency-based price differential is temporarily propping up our ailing automakers by making their competitor's products much more expensive. As a result, this is also creating a serious surge of inflation because many Americans are still buying large quantities of foreign products that now cost much more than they did just a few years ago.

Given the weak dollar, American automobiles should be selling at significantly lower prices than the Japanese or German imports. However GM and Ford products are not less expensive. The truth is that they are barely competitive, losing market share, and struggling just to stay alive. If American manufacturers like the auto industry have to carry the extra cost of healthcare – costs that their competitors do not have - they may soon disappear. Every year, more American jobs are lost – and they are not coming back!

Clearly, the cost of healthcare is not the only reason that American jobs are racing to other countries. However, it is definitely one of the big ones! Every other major industrialized nation is driving on the other side of Healthcare Boulevard, by providing National Healthcare. What should we do about that?

All of the studies and statistics show that Americans pay nearly twice as much for healthcare than the citizens of other advanced countries. If our healthcare was significantly better than theirs, it could be argued that it would be worth the extra cost, but it is not!

In 2004, the Commonwealth Fund compiled the first international report that compared the healthcare quality in twenty-nine advanced countries, including the United States. It showed that the U.S. healthcare was not nearly as good as many of the other countries, but that Americans paid nearly twice as much as other countries for their mediocre healthcare.[2]

The New England Journal of Medicine is the most respected source of information about our country's $2 trillion a year healthcare industry. It reported in March 2006 that, incredibly, U.S. patients receive the proper medical care from doctors and nurses only 55% of the time from our "fragmented and chaotic" healthcare system![3] Paying twice the worldwide rate for that kind of healthcare is not only ridiculous, it is also downright scary.

## A BRIEF HISTORY OF AMERICAN HEALTHCARE

Waiting to get a haircut recently, I picked up a book about the history of American barbers. I read that George Washington died in the arms of his barber who was bloodletting the former president as the "medical" way to deal with a sickness he had contracted. At that time, barbers were on America's front line of healthcare delivery. The red, white and blue stripes on a barber's pole represented blood, bandages and veins. The brass bowl on the top of the pole was used to keep leeches for extracting blood. Washington died from that procedure while he was personally monitoring his own pulse. That was the state of the art in medicine at that time when things were rather simple.

Eventually, doctors and medical licenses regulated the barbers to simply cutting hair. There are, however, very valuable lessons to be learned for the leaders of our country from that episode in American medical history. No matter how well the intentions, or how "right" some people thought that bloodletting was, when it was discovered that it was doing more harm than good, they stopped doing it!

WHETHER IT WAS SUICIDAL PROTECTIONIST POLICIES FOR DETROIT, OR "WELFARE CRACK" FOR THE POOR, THE MODERN DEMOCRATIC PARTY WAS NOW IGNORING ITS NOBLE AND PROUD TRADITIONS, AND INSTEAD IT HAD BEGUN SELLING ITS SOUL FOR SPECIAL INTEREST VOTES.

In more recent history, however, our political leaders have failed to correct obvious mistakes. For example in the late 1960's, the great democratic senator from New York, Patrick Daniel Moynihan preached endlessly that the large menu of welfare programs for single mothers was going to destroy the black family unit, which of course it quickly did.

Moynihan was ostracized by his fellow Democrats who had quickly learned that as long as Black Americans were dependant upon them to continue to deliver the welfare benefits, they would remain a solid voting bloc for Democrats. That is why ghettos, entitlements, and other social ills are so permanent. Whether it was suicidal protectionist policies for Detroit, or "welfare crack" for the poor, the modern Democratic Party was now ignoring its noble and proud traditions, and instead it had begun selling its soul for special interest votes. Like piglets on a sow, several other healthcare special interest groups soon learned how to fatten themselves up on the country's $2 trillion a year healthcare system.

Just as with energy, more than one president (both Republican and Democrat) had unsuccessfully tried to plug the holes in the country's healthcare bucket. They were, however, hog-tied and disposed of in short order by the special interest groups and their hired hands, selected U.S. Congressmen.

## HEALTHCARE LEGISLATION PRE-BILL CLINTON

In 1911, following Germany's lead, Britain instituted its National Insurance Act. Shortly thereafter, the American Association for Labor Legislation (AALL) lobbied for a plan that would combine the best of the German and British plans. Unfortunately, there was not a David Lloyd George or an Otto von Bismarck on the American side of the Atlantic.

The quest for a national healthcare plan, one that would guarantee every American citizen the peace of mind of knowing that his or her family would have access to not just food, water, air and shelter, but also to basic medical necessities, would continue decade after decade into the future.

## Franklin Roosevelt — (1933 - 1945)

In 1938, President Franklin Roosevelt sent the National Health Plan to Congress for "careful study"; however, the events leading up to World War II had already begun to draw all of the congressional attention. FDR tested the water and determined that he would fight (and did) other battles, such as Social Security. The resulting "New Deal" was the largest federal involvement into the everyday lives of Americans in the country's history. Securing national healthcare would have to fall to a future president.

## Harry Truman — (1945 - 1953)

Harry Truman was the first president to actively pursue legislation that would have required coverage for all Americans. However, the "three pigs" (the trial lawyers association, the insurance companies, and the American Medical Association [AMA]), who were extracting huge sums of money from America's healthcare resources, were not about to give up their gravy train without a fight.

Lawyers, lobbyists and their lackey legislators

144

immediately went to work with an advertising blitzkrieg and quickly outmaneuvered the unprepared Truman. The three pigs were now able to go back and fatten up in peace and quiet for awhile.

## Dwight Eisenhower — (1953 - 1961)

In 1953, President Eisenhower spoke to the House Ways and Means Committee about his thoughts on national healthcare. In a burst of compassion, he stated "If all that Americans want is security, they can go to prison. They'll have enough to eat, a bed, and a roof over their heads." The committee members must have assumed that meant the president would not be offering legislation to provide Americans who were not in jail with any type of basic healthcare coverage.[4]

> ... "IF ALL THAT AMERICANS WANT IS SECURITY, THEY CAN GO TO PRISON. THEY'LL HAVE ENOUGH TO EAT, A BED, AND A ROOF OVER THEIR HEADS."

## John Kennedy — (1961 - 1963)

John Kennedy's campaign platform included a Medicare proposal that would help those that were "too old to work and ... too young to die."[5] The new president lobbied hard to build a base of public and congressional support. He was still actively pursuing an old age medical bill when he was assassinated.

## Lyndon Johnson — (1963 - 1969)

It should come as no surprise that the first major victories in the fight for a national health plan were won by Lyndon Johnson. America's all-time legislative leader picked what he considered the two most critical areas of healthcare concern (the elderly and the poor) and included them in his *Great Society* bundle of legislation. For the first time, Medicare and Medicaid provided those two large segments of the American population the guarantee of a basic right: the right to not feel helpless and hopeless in the face of a medical crisis.

This was a defining moment for the Democratic Party — a high-water mark — and a moment to be proud. Future mismanagement and abuse eventually caused many Americans to question the wisdom of passing these programs. However, even minor reflection reveals that

> THIS WAS A DEFINING MOMENT FOR THE DEMOCRATIC PARTY — A HIGH-WATER MARK — AND A MOMENT TO BE PROUD.

mismanagement and abuse are the problems — not the question of whether or not we should protect our most vulnerable citizens.

## Richard Nixon — (1969 - 1974)

When Richard Nixon became president, it marked a turning point in the saga of comprehensive national health insurance. Now Republicans would join in the push to provide medical coverage for all Americans. On February 6, 1974, President Nixon introduced CHIP (Comprehensive Health Insurance Plan) and proclaimed that national health insurance was "an idea whose time has come in America."[6] Soon, however, the events of Watergate would swamp any legislative push for comprehensive healthcare during the Nixon administration.

## Gerald Ford — (1974 - 1977)

When Gerald Ford assumed the office of the presidency after Richard Nixon's resignation, he surprised many people when he immediately began to promote the idea of enacting a national health insurance plan. He contributed to an article in the New York Times and stated that it was a "sad commentary" that Congress had avoided the issue of national health reform for more than 25 years.[7]

The trial lawyers, insurance companies, and the American Medical Association went on high alert. The three pigs went right to work in an attempt to maintain their ability to milk the system at everyone else's expense.

Like many of the presidents before him, Ford was threatening to huff and puff and blow down the house of the three pigs. However, they joined forces along with their lobbyists and their congressional indentured servants. Together, they withstood yet another attempt to separate them from the hundreds of billions of non-healthcare dollars that they siphoned each year from the existing healthcare system.

President Ford made only minor headway in the fight to reduce needless extra healthcare costs that could have enabled Congress to redirect those savings into actual healthcare expenses. He did get the HMO Act passed, but that was merely a little straw off the roof of the three pigs' house. Substantive change was attempted but not achieved during the eight years of the Nixon/Ford administration.

## Jimmy Carter — (1977 - 1981)

From 1968 to 1976, the Democrats controlled both houses of Congress and the Republicans controlled the presidency (Nixon/Ford). Many times, partisan divisions can greatly inhibit the passage of monumental legislation such as healthcare. However in 1976, the Democrats won control of all three legs of the legislative stool. These were the same circumstances that allowed Lyndon Johnson to figuratively qualify for the legislative hall of fame.

Unfortunately, despite a personal Herculean effort, Carter's attempt at comprehensive national healthcare reform met the same fate as his comprehensive energy plan.

This happened primarily because of two key reasons. First and foremost, Jimmy Carter lacked leadership skills.

Secondly, Ted Kennedy intended to (and did) challenge Carter for the 1980 democratic presidential nomination. Kennedy undermined Carter on many issues including healthcare, which he wanted to use himself as an election issue if he got the nomination. Carter was no match for the three pigs and Ted Kennedy.

The four years of the Carter presidency were the best potential opportunity to resolve the medical delivery system in the U.S. for several years to come. Dr. Kimberly Weathers, who did extensive research on Carter's ill-fated healthcare attempt, summed it up as follows: "The story of national health insurance under the Carter administration is one of confusion, frustration, and ultimately, complete failure."[8] Carter himself said that failure was "the greatest disappointment of my presidency."[9]

> ... "The story of national health insurance under the Carter administration is one of confusion, frustration, and ultimately, complete failure."

## Ronald Reagan and George H.W. Bush

In the twelve years that followed Jimmy Carter, Republicans Ronald Reagan and George H.W. Bush took healthcare off of the front burner, skipped the back burner and moved it off of the stove entirely. Other than extending Medicare (an existing program) and passing a few minor bills that were little more than window dressing, the Republicans had no interest in expanding the role or size of the federal government.

The Republicans believed strongly that the outrageous fraud, waste and abuse that was rampant in nearly all federal undertakings, including Medicare and Medicaid, was more than enough reason to not let the government get a hold of another potential boondoggle. Their logic was sound.

However, the current system was broken, wasting hundreds of billions of dollars every year, providing second rate service to millions of Americans, causing millions of jobs to move to other countries, and leaving tens of millions of Americans with no insurance at all. Ignoring those facts was illogical.

## THE LONG ROAD LED TO BILL CLINTON

Sometimes in our personal lives, in the fortunes of a company, or in the apparent destiny of a country, things can seem to come together all at once. What may have seemed remote, out of reach, or even impossible suddenly appears to be reality unfolding; and so it was in 1992 for the proponents of a comprehensive national healthcare plan for all Americans. Once again, the Democrats gained control of the presidency and both houses of Congress by a wide margin. Bill Clinton made healthcare reform one of his major campaign pledges, and he was personally committed to its enactment.

For him, it was not just a convenient campaign issue that would be forgotten after the election. He fully intended to finally round up the hundreds of uncoordinated, inefficient, and incomplete pieces of the American healthcare system and meld them into a cohesive, cost effective and comprehensive system that would be superior to any other system in any other country. It would be ours, and it would be the best!

Furthermore, Bill Clinton was not Jimmy Carter. No, we were told that he was highly intelligent, energetic and oozing with charisma. He would be that special politician that only comes along every now and then, the democratic equivalent of a Ronald Reagan.

The clouds parted, and the sun, the stars, the moon and the planets were now all in alignment. The elusive goal of resolving the country's healthcare issues was at last ripe, within reach, and ready to be picked. It was hanging so low that Clinton would not even need a ladder to reach it. All he had to do was execute!

*The United States is the only advanced country in the world without a national healthcare plan. In the first year of the Clinton-Gore Administration, that will change.*

— PUTTING PEOPLE FIRST, CLINTON/GORE, 1992

## PICK A STRATEGY

Bill Clinton was fortunate to have the luxury of studying the last two democratic presidents. Because Lyndon Johnson and Jimmy Carter's styles were so completely different, as were their legislative achievements, it offered the new president an excellent opportunity to assess the lessons learned from both of his most recent democratic predecessors. Surely common sense dictated that he would examine their successes and failures in order to help himself prepare an intelligent strategy for what he said would be the centerpiece of legislative agenda: comprehensive national healthcare.

HE DID NOT OPT FOR ONLY PART OF IT, OR EVEN MOST OF IT. HE CHOSE TO REPEAT EACH AND EVERY PAINFUL MISTAKE THAT CARTER HAD MADE WHEN HE ATTEMPTED TO SECURE PASSAGE OF HIS ENERGY PROPOSAL.

Unfortunately, Bill Clinton was very much like Jimmy Carter when it came to learning from past presidents. Carter was always certain that he was right and that every one else should do what he said simply

152

because he had said it. They never understood why that was not enough.

Incredibly, unbelievably, bizarrely and without explanation, Bill Clinton knowingly or unknowingly duplicated Jimmy Carter's flawed legislative strategy in order to attempt the enactment of his own healthcare initiative. He did not opt for only part of it or even most of it. He chose to repeat each and every painful mistake that Carter had made when he attempted to secure passage of his energy proposal. What was Bill Clinton thinking?

## THE BEGINNING OF THE END

After the election in 1992, the liberal wing of the Democratic Party was giddy with anticipation. Surely, many new social programs and policies would soon be rolling off of the legislative assembly line. In the grand tradition of Franklin Roosevelt and Lyndon Johnson, the Democrats were now in a position to actively address the growing list of important issues that had been accumulating for decades. That, of course, would include healthcare. Given that Lyndon Johnson was not naturally gifted with charisma and only possessed limited inspirational leadership skills, it was possible that a dynamic figure like Bill Clinton could be headed for Mount Rushmore.

## "HEY, HE FORGOT TO TOUCH FIRST BASE!"

It is important to remember that, after the 1992 election, even though the Democrats won large majorities in both the House and the Senate, Bill Clinton won the presidency with less than half of the popular vote (43%). Ross Perot's candidacy was a real factor and that meant that Clinton had not yet connected with even half of the American voters. Leadership expert James MacGregor Burns noted, "The Clinton's most egregious failure was in educating the public. Clinton's hubris was a failure to recognize that his mastery and belief in his political and policy understandings is not the same as the public understanding."[10]

RESPONDING TO QUESTIONS ABOUT HER FULL-TIME POLITICAL INVOLVEMENT, SHE STATED THAT SHE COULD INSTEAD "HAVE STAYED HOME AND BAKED COOKIES AND HAD TEAS."

Building a solid base of support for an issue during the presidential campaign, with both the public and the Congress (especially by helping to campaign for fellow Democrats who were also running for election), is the crucial first step in passing a monumental piece of legislation. This did not happen in 1992. Bill Clinton was too busy trying to explain away allegations about several illicit affairs and other non-policy items.

Hillary Clinton, the key player in the upcoming healthcare battle, was inadvertently alienating millions of traditional stay-at-home moms. Responding to questions about her full-time political involvement, she stated that she could instead "have stayed home and baked cookies and had teas."[11]

While Hillary was the darling of her like minded friends, she had quickly managed to alienate a large segment of the American people. Whether some people were awestruck or ticked off, the indisputable fact was that there was a large ground swell of vehement disdain and opposition. Many people had a visceral reaction and quickly came to dislike the Clintons on a personal level. The degree of hostility and polarization was unprecedented. The continual references to "Slick Willie" and "Hillary the Horrible" had taken political discourse to a new low and detracted from the necessary political discussion.

Neither Richard Nixon nor Jimmy Carter had even re-motely generated the intense level of personal animosity that had developed in the Clinton's detractors and critics. That deep gulf of social division and constant generation of negative energy has persisted to this day. Today, the Bush haters have taken their turn to spew venom. For the prior eight years, it had been the Clinton haters. When will it end?

During the campaign when a future president should be laying a solid foundation of public and congressional support, the Clintons were busy attempting to explain away allegations of past indiscretions and many people's perception of their elitist attitude. This energized their opposition.

Healthcare was mentioned during the campaign, but it was lost in the many conversations about Bill's alleged prior sexual affairs and Hillary's disdain for the role of a traditional homemaker. Jennifer Flowers, an alleged long-time girlfriend of Bill Clinton, was probably mentioned more often than national healthcare.

## "HEY, HE FORGOT TO TOUCH SECOND BASE!"

After winning the election, President-elect Clinton was strongly advised (begged) by Vice President Al Gore, House Speaker Tom Foley, House Majority Leader Richard Gephardt, and Senate Majority Leader George Mitchell not to alienate his administration from Congress as Jimmy Carter had done and to avoid another James Schlesinger episode.[12]

Despite massive advice to the contrary, on January 25, 1993, Bill Clinton announced that he was setting up a new task force to address the upcoming healthcare initiative. Instead of being inclusive and asking congressional leaders for their input as well as asking them to assign people to work on the task force (which would be giving those key players a stake in the development of the plan), Clinton informed them that Hillary Rodham Clinton was in charge and that, essentially, she would be running the show.

Hillary did include a few token congressional appointees to the task force but not the key players and not nearly enough to make Congress feel as though they were a major player or partner. Leadership scholars Georgia Sorenson and James MacGregor Burns have written, "The failure to recognize allies, to build alliances, where needed, to understand the power of the wholly entrenched Democratic leadership in Congress, emerged as a fundamental leadership failure on the part of the President."[13]

OFF TO A GLORIOUS START, THE CLINTONS WERE ABOUT TO GO "ALL IN" WITH THE HAND THAT THEY INTENDED TO PLAY.

Now Congress (especially the leadership) had its ego needlessly bruised by this baffling blunder. Off to a glorious start, the Clintons were about to go "all in" with the hand that they intended to play. Secret, and perhaps illegal, behind closed door meetings that excluded everyone but Hillary's hand picked confidants became the selected strategy of choice. There was not a warm and fuzzy feeling that enveloped this affair. The public, not to mention Congress, did not appreciate the condescension and the superior attitude that was seemingly being shoved in their faces.

The media was angered by the fact that they were not allowed to attend the secret "open government" meetings. Worse still, members of Hillary's task force thought that they could periodically throw the media a few selected news crumbs and that the peasants of the press would be satisfied. Well, not quite! Sorenson and Burns also wrote, "The press resented the spoon-feeding of administration pablum on healthcare from low-level White House staff."[14]

WHY POKE YOUR OPPONENTS WITH A STICK AND MAKE THEM EVEN MORE DIFFICULT TO DEAL WITH?

A critical mistake was also excluding the special interest groups (the three pigs) who undoubtedly became paranoid about the secret meetings and their lack of inclusion. The trial lawyers, the insurance companies, the American Hospital Association and the AMA had been a huge part of America's healthcare system for decades. Even if someone (including this writer) felt that they were more of the problem than the solution, certainly these key players should have been given a chance to have input (and maybe make concessions willingly) during the process. Why poke your opponents with a stick and make them even more difficult to deal with?

## "HEY, HE'S OUTSIDE OF THE BASE PATH!"

With their sirens blaring and red lights flashing, the three pigs sprang into action. However, they were running a little slower these days because they had gotten quite fat by milking the system for so many years. The hundreds of billions of dollars that they siphoned off of the healthcare industry each year were once again at risk, and as usual they were going to pull out all of the stops in order to prevent losing their healthcare feast. However, the three pigs did not really have to worry. This would be the easiest defense that they would ever have to mount.

The good news for the three pigs was that Bill Clinton was going to unknowingly help their defense by appointing his wife as the figurehead of his healthcare task force. Instantly, half of the American people were against the plan, no matter what it would eventually look like. "Hillarycare" allowed opponents to personify the plan with a person who had, for whatever reason, generated an intense negative reaction in many people. If she proposed it, half of the country would reject it, because the red/blue divide was now clearly in play. Did Bill Clinton ever consider that?

## HOW DO YOU SPELL SIMPLE?

In an awesome display of disconnect, Hillary Rodham Clinton proudly presented a massive and incredibly complex 1,342 page healthcare document that she fully expected would impress anyone who saw it or even heard about it. One staffer boasted that the plan had over 800 movable parts.

Did she really think that 535 congressmen would actually read it, understand it, debate it and then vote for it?

Perhaps she thought that because it had her name on it, congressmen would simply forego the formalities of proper procedure, accept it on faith, and just pass it. Anybody's guess is as good as anyone else's because it defied any common sense explanation.

... "HOW DO YOU REMOVE YOUR SUPPORT IF YOUR SPOUSE DOES A LOUSY JOB?"

Now Bill Clinton was really in a jam. In the same way that President Carter had unwisely turned the destiny of his energy plan over to someone else (James Schlesinger) and lost control of the situation, President Clinton was helplessly watching Hillary, like a bull in a china shop, destroy any possible chance of passing a comprehensive national healthcare plan. The Ways and Means Staff Director, David Abernethy lamented, "How do you remove your support if your spouse does a lousy job?"[15]

## "HEY, HE MISSED THIRD BASE!"

An easy lesson to learn (they are all easy if you pay attention) from Carter's energy debacle was that "Hannibal Jerkin" (Hamilton Jordan) and the inexperienced staff from Georgia had needlessly rubbed all of the right people the wrong way. An arrogant and abrasive staff could seriously undermine the working relationships with key congressional leaders.

Ira Magaziner was an old friend of the Clintons. He was

also an avid Star Trek fan but totally inexperienced in the ways of Washington and healthcare. For some unknown reason, he was appointed as the head administrator and architect of Hillary's healthcare plan. In 1992, *The New Republic* reported that Magaziner was "a social planner with an unbounded faith in ... grandiose systems."[16] Boy, they weren't kidding!

> ... "A SOCIAL PLANNER WITH AN UNBOUNDED FAITH IN ... GRANDIOSE SYSTEMS"

Magaziner's constant references to congressional leaders as "you guys" clearly exposed an attitude problem that permeated the task force.[17] The congressmen were not amused. Democratic Chairman of the powerful House Ways and Means Committee and Clinton supporter, Dan Rostenkowski, complained, "Those guys (the Clintons) get in there and think they know it all."[18]

Compromise, give and take, negotiation, and "half a loaf is better than no loaf," are familiar terms. Everyone knows that there is a reason that the founding fathers created a House of Representatives, a Senate and the office of the president. While it would have been easier to just have a king, they thought that representative government that allowed input from all corners of the republic would be the best and fairest type of government.

> ... "THOSE GUYS (THE CLINTONS) GET IN THERE AND THINK THEY KNOW IT ALL"

That, of course, implied there would be an opportunity for different ideas, opinions and adjustments to accommodate the various interests and factions. Washington is the quintessential town of horse trading. Why did Bill Clinton not understand that?

Other democratic congressmen offered different versions of healthcare that actually had greater congressional support and thus a greater chance of passing than the "Hillarycare" plan. Jim Cooper (D-Tennessee) offered a compromise plan that eliminated the controversial mandates for employers. Jim McDermott (D-Washington) offered a compromise single-payer (federal government) plan that had **90 congressional co-sponsors**. That was a plan that actually had an excellent chance to pass. The Clinton response was essentially, "It's my way or no way!" So "no way" it would be.

Despite the pledge to produce a healthcare bill in the first 100 days of the Clinton presidency, it was closer to two years before "Hillarycare" was ready to go to a vote. This, of course, meant that the presidential legislative honeymoon period was a thing of the past and, more importantly, that midterm elections were approaching. Congressmen would now only be concerned how their vote on a bill would affect their re-election — not if it was a good bill (How do you spell TERM LIMITS?).

Along with an unconvinced public, hostile special interest groups, alienated congressmen, a disgruntled media, a bill so complex that no one really had any idea what it meant, obnoxious staffers ticking off key players, and incredibly poor timing, the bill also had a lighting rod of controversy as its figurehead — and she was not open to compromise. In other words, it was a legislative nightmare!

## TAGGED AT THE PLATE - "YOU'RE OUT!"

"Hillarycare" had virtually no chance of getting passed. Democratic congressmen pleaded for it not to be put to a vote because they did not want to vote for such a convoluted piece of legislation, and they also did not want to embarrass their democratic president. Making his first good decision on the bill since the process began during the campaign more than two years before, Clinton, without even making an appearance, released an announcement, "This journey **is** far, far from over … we are going to keep up the fight and we will prevail."[19]

Perhaps some Americans did not know what the meaning of the word "is" is because despite the announcement, the Clintons never attempted to pass a comprehensive healthcare plan again. The last six years of the Clinton co-presidency did pass a few small piecemeal healthcare

*When I have fully decided that a result is worth getting I go ahead on it and make trial after trial until it comes.*

— THOMAS A. EDISON

measures. They did stick a few more wads of gum in the leaking dam. However by 1994, the last best opportunity that our country had at solving one of our biggest problems had been missed because of hubris and ineptitude.

David Walker recently resigned as the chief of the General Accounting Office (GAO) of the United States government. He was the top accountant for our country's fiscal affairs. He is now touring the country trying to alert us that we heading for bankruptcy unless there are many major changes made to our nation's finances. He says that **healthcare costs are problem number one**!

Jimmy Carter carried the energy torch, but it fell to the ground. It is still burning, but it has been lying on the ground for nearly thirty years. Bill Clinton carried the healthcare torch, but it, too, fell to the ground. It is still burning, but it has been lying on the ground for fourteen years. Our country is losing millions of jobs and even entire industries (will automobiles be next?) partly because of these two problems. Where is a president who will pick up the torches?

■  ▩  ■

*Adversity weakens the weak and strengthens the strong.*

— ANONYMOUS

## CHAPTER SIX

# AUTHOR'S
# REFLECTIONS
# &
# LESSONS
# LEARNED

*Destiny is not a matter of chance, it is matter of choice; it is not a thing to be waited for, it is a thing to be achieved.*

— WILLIAM JENNINGS BRYAN
THREE-TIME DEMOCRATIC NOMINEE FOR THE U.S. PRESIDENCY, 1860-1925

## REFLECTIONS

As a private citizen, I have spent the last four years researching this book. Ironically, four major points or "lessons learned" became apparent. Each has had a profound impact on my thinking, my perspective of these four presidents, and how they relate to the future of our country. A full range of emotional reactions developed as I researched each of the four legislative attempts. Appreciation and frustration seem to dominate, but anger was also recurrent, as were rushes of patriotic pride. It was an experience that I will always remember.

My source of inspiration was Thomas Paine who, as a private citizen, wrote *Common Sense*. That fifty page pamphlet became the tipping point of public opinion in the debate about declaring America's independence from England. Hundreds of thousands of the small books were purchased in the thirteen colonies. The logical arguments for breaking ties with England were simple but compelling and thus "common sense."

Just as today, public opinion at that time was nearly

evenly split. Then the debate was whether to remain loyal to the British Crown or to form a new republic. As a private citizen, Thomas Paine made a difference, perhaps **the** difference, in that historic debate. Drawing on his spirit and sense of possibility, I hope that when you have read this book, it may have helped you think a little more about what was done, and what else could have been done, regarding the four important presidential initiatives that were reviewed.

> AS A PRIVATE CITIZEN, THOMAS PAINE MADE A DIFFERENCE, PERHAPS **THE** DIFFERENCE, IN THAT HISTORIC DEBATE.

More importantly, however, maybe the lessons that we learned will be applied to many other important issues that are facing our country. Other private citizens, such as you, may become motivated to make a contribution, such as writing a book, running for office, or volunteering some time to a worthy cause, etc. Certainly 535 congressmen and one president are not going to solve the majority of our country's problems. We are! Democracy is a participant sport. We can't win the game sitting on the bench or sitting in the bleachers. Let's get up and go do something!

## THE FIRST LESSON LEARNED

As simple as it may seem, there is clearly a very important checklist of dos and don'ts that a president must be aware of if he or she intends to pass a significant piece of legislation. There were ten common factors that were present in all four of the examples that were examined. They all seem to be items in which "common sense" would dictate the appropriate choices, actions or strategies, but that was clearly not the case for Presidents Carter and Clinton. Not surprisingly, Kennedy and Johnson successfully handled each of the ten factors one way, and Carter and Clinton did the opposite — with the opposite result!

## THE TEN PRESIDENTIAL CHECKLIST ITEMS:

1. During the campaign, a presidential candidate must establish with the public a solid base of support for the issue that will be subsequently submitted as a major piece of legislation. That support will provide pressure on congressmen. Kennedy clearly sold the public on the need for America to challenge the Russians in space. Johnson convinced most Americans that he should carry out the unfinished agenda of John Kennedy. Carter mentioned energy and Clinton mentioned healthcare during their campaigns, but neither were able to generate a large ground

swell of public support that would create the momentum to push their legislation.

2. Unlike Kennedy and Johnson who were formerly Senators, Carter and Clinton ran their campaigns as Washington outsiders, which they were. Both were small state southern governors who railed against the Washington establishment, belittled the Congress and blasted the special interest groups. It was a great campaign tactic; however, it was a poor strategy to use in preparations for attempting to pass major legislation. They would soon need the Washington establishment, the Congress and at least some degree of cooperation from some of the special interest groups.

3. Carter and Clinton also failed to help democratic congressional candidates ride their coat tails. If elected, they owed the president nothing! This was not a strong point for Kennedy either. However, Johnson wrote the book on how to create a bank of political favors that were owed and could be cashed out in the future.

4. Elitism, secret meetings, and condescension were poison in the Carter and Clinton episodes. Inclusion, respect, and common sense worked very well for Johnson and Kennedy.

5. Intelligently choosing the best person to lead the proposal and knowing that person will be subconsciously identified with it is critical. Kennedy astutely chose Johnson to head up the Apollo program, and Johnson chose himself to shepherd his *Great Society* legislation. Unfortunately, James Schlesinger and Hillary Clinton were the male and female versions of the smart person that many people also found to be obnoxious and abrasive.

6. Effectively giving up control of the issues to James Schlesinger and Hillary Rodham Clinton left both Presidents Carter and Clinton in a position from which there was no room to retreat and regroup. That was never a problem for either Kennedy or Johnson.

7. During the Kennedy and Johnson administrations, key interest groups were first identified and then systematically included in the process as stakeholders, so they might become more likely to be supportive of the administration's proposal. Jimmy Carter and Bill Clinton never seemed to understand this basic concept.

8. Making sure that the people in your organization have good people skills and have basic common

sense seems so fundamental that it feels funny even writing about it. However, contrasting the professionalism of Lawrence O'Brien (he was the head of the Organization of Congressional Relations for both Kennedy and Johnson) with "Hannibal Jerkin" and Ira Magaziner, makes you scratch your head and wonder out loud, "What were Carter and Clinton thinking?"

9. Kennedy and Johnson were both excellent negotiators; and they were ready, willing and able to compromise if necessary to get the bulk of their agenda enacted. Perhaps Carter and Clinton had been able to bulldoze the Georgia and Arkansas legislatures, but that did not play well in Washington. Johnson once said, "Frequently in life I have had to settle for progress short of perfection. I have done so because — despite the cynics — I believe that half a loaf is better than none … and if I go on working, the day of the full loaf will come."[1]

> ... I BELIEVE THAT HALF A LOAF IS BETTER THAN NONE ... AND IF I GO ON WORKING, THE DAY OF THE FULL LOAF WILL COME"

10. By the time Kennedy and Johnson had already accomplished the majority of their agendas, Carter and Clinton were still asking for directions to the White House. Timing is critical at many different steps in the legislative process; unfortunately, Bill and Jimmy never saw the need to wear a watch.

It has been more than forty years since Lyndon Johnson broke the legislative logjam in Washington, and he was able to deal with dozens of America's serious issues that had been accumulating for decades. That brings to mind the next lesson learned.

## THE SECOND LESSON LEARNED

Of all of the hundreds of quotes that I read while doing this research, the one that struck me the most was uttered by Lyndon Johnson. Shortly after winning the 1964 election, President Johnson sighed deeply and said, "Everything on my desk today was here when I first came to Congress" which was more than twenty-six years before.[2] There are long periods in American history when many problems accumulate and only a few are resolved.

There have been eight presidents since Lyndon Johnson. I believe that most Americans would agree that in our increasingly complex and ever changing world unresolved issues have been accumulating at an alarming rate during all of those administrations.

An exodus of American jobs and entire industries to foreign countries, immigration, trade deficits, budget deficits, energy dependence, educational decline, healthcare problems, threats of terrorism, our huge and growing debt to foreign countries, tremendous funding shortfalls (for Social Security, Medicare, and Medicaid, etc.), crumbling infrastructure (roads, bridges, and power grids), crime, a tax system that is a mindless patchwork of endless regulations and which costs nearly $150 billion a year just to administrate, no national plan to manage our water supply, a U.S. dollar that is constantly losing value in the world marketplace, and millions of undereducated - and thus unemployable - American workers who lack the basic job skills that are necessary in today's increasingly technological world are just **some** of the major issues that await the next president.

It is hard to understand why anyone would want the job! Fortunately, there are still some Americans who are willing to run for president. But what will happen after they have been elected? Hopefully they will have read this and many other books and by studying past presidential actions, it may assist them to actually get their agenda enacted.

We cannot afford repeats of the energy and healthcare fiascos. There are dozens of important issues that

WE CANNOT AFFORD REPEATS OF THE ENERGY AND HEALTHCARE FIASCOS.

must be resolved and resolved quickly. The longer we wait, the more difficult it will be to do what needs to be done.

## THE THIRD LESSON LEARNED

Each of the four presidents brought a different but very valuable leadership skill to the table. There are four major leadership lessons to be learned (one apiece) from each of these presidents that will be invaluable to future presidents — if he or she takes the time to learn them!

## PRESIDENT KENNEDY

*Leaders establish the vision for the future and set the strategy for getting there.*

— JOHN P. KOTTER, HARVARD BUSINESS SCHOOL

John Kennedy showed us that we could and should look to the future. He made Americans realize that the future was something that we could, at least to some degree, create, rather than something that was simply going to happen to us. He had vision, **AND** the ability to empower many Americans to also share his vision. Furthermore, he was able to motivate and inspire citizens to welcome and embrace change and make it happen. He was a transformational leader whose leadership motivated people — not just someone who passed legislation.

Any future president who expects to have a major impact on the outlook and outcomes of our country, better be able to arouse and inspire the positive energy and good-will of the American people. We now know what that looks like.

**Thank you John Kennedy!**

## PRESIDENT JOHNSON

*A genuine leader is not a searcher for consensus
but a molder of consensus.*

— MARTIN LUTHER KING, JR.

Lyndon Johnson clearly showed us that after all of the election parties are over, there is still the challenge of actually making your agenda become a reality for the American people. More than perhaps any president in American history, Johnson demonstrated that there are many different leadership skills that can be learned, utilized and perfected. While Kennedy's strong suit was transformational or inspirational leadership, Johnson excelled at the one on one, everyday back and forth, traditional style of leadership that comes with years of practice and effort.

However, like a baseball pitcher who wanted to add one more pitch to his bag of tricks, Johnson was willing to step out of his comfort zone, and he attempted to add transformational leadership skills to his arsenal. While he was not as effective as John Kennedy, he did successfully achieve some additional support by appealing to some people's higher sense of motivation. This was especially true when he was pushing for the Civil Rights Act and the Voting Rights Act. He believed strongly in the moral correctness of those bills, and he let his personal passion help carry the day.

We now know that presidential leadership is comprised of a large set of leadership skills. A president must make a deliberate point of acquiring those skills. Then they must be finely tuned, and constantly honed. Knowing which skill to use in a given circumstance is a skill all its own. Like watching a chef putting on a cooking demonstration, a study of presidential leadership in 1965 and 1966 reveals the entire range of leadership skills that any president will probably ever need. When the demonstration was over, there was not one pot or pan that had not been used.

**Thank you Lyndon Johnson!**

## PRESIDENT CARTER

*Nothing in the world can take the place of persistence. Talent will not; nothing is more common than unsuccessful men with talent. Genius will not; unrewarded genius is almost a proverb. Education will not; the world is full of educated derelicts. Persistence and determination alone are omnipotent.*

— CALVIN COOLIDGE

We all realize that no matter how weak or strong a president might be, the going many times becomes rough and tough. Trying to juggle numerous issues, the media, congressmen, special interest groups, staff, fickle and impatient voters, as well as a major crisis or two that can crop up which is completely out of your control, can easily overwhelm even the most disciplined individual. Yet, a president must balance it all AND KEEP GOING!

Jimmy Carter's strongest asset was his ability to stay the course and keep at it. When his energy program was defeated, he came back with another one. His tenacity was definitely something to admire. While Carter did have some legislative successes, he was usually climbing up a very steep hill. For four years, he climbed continuously despite setbacks, a hostile media, the Iranian hostage crisis, and a souring mood of the American people.

Given the long list of incredibly significant issues that are piled high waiting for the next president, it is clear that perseverance, dogged determination, and tenacity will be an absolute requirement. We now know what that looks like.

**Thank you Jimmy Carter!**

## PRESIDENT CLINTON

*In the field of world policy I would dedicate this nation to the policy of the good neighbor.*
— FRANKLIN D. ROOSEVELT, FIRST INAUGURAL ADDRESS

The oceans that used to separate, protect and, to some degree, isolate America from the rest of the world, are now merely puddles in the international neighborhood. Our country is a member of the world community, and every other country is our neighbor. Being a good neighbor is as American as apple pie, fireworks, and baseball.

Bill Clinton's major contribution as president was being a great American ambassador to the world. In the mid 1990's he worked diligently to try and bring peace to Ireland. The Catholics and Protestants had been busy terrorizing and killing each other for many years. By helping to orchestrate the Good Friday Peace Accord, he was a major factor in working for, and in fact achieving, a real cease fire.

His efforts and commitment were not lost on the Irish people. At a huge rally in Belfast, thousands of people came together to celebrate and hundreds of them were waving American flags. Whether you were a Democrat, a Republican or someone who was too lazy to even vote; if you were still breathing you could not help but well up with pride and have a mega-dose of American patriotism racing through your veins.

It was an awesome display of presidential leadership that effectively serves as a reminder of what is possible for America on the international scene.

**Thank you Bill Clinton!**

The third lesson learned is that the epitome of a modern presidential leader would be someone who has a clear vision, arouses the imagination and energy of the American people to follow that vision, has the leadership skills to enact the vision into successful legislation, has the perseverance and determination to see it through and make necessary adjustments along the way, and who can work and interact with our world neighbors in a spirit of mutual respect and cooperation. We have seen all of these attributes, yet not in one president. However, now we know who we are looking for.

**Where is Lyndon "Billy Jim" Kennedy?**

## THE FOURTH AND FINAL LESSON LEARNED

Like many other Americans, I personally felt that the country suffered a major loss when Bill Clinton's attempt to pass a comprehensive healthcare plan failed. While many of us did not particularly like the "Hillarycare" plan, the fact remains that our healthcare bucket still has a hundred holes in it. The trial lawyers, insurance companies and the AMA tell us we need to just keep pouring the money in faster.

The three pigs are now lying under the bucket, on their backs, hands behind their heads, with their mouths wide open and the money just keeps flowing. Fourteen years later, we are still the only advanced major country that does not have a national healthcare plan — and our jobs keep leaving our country for those foreign destinations. Look out! Look out! We are driving on the wrong side of the Healthcare Boulevard!

However as huge as that loss was, it was small compared to all of the other things that did not happen as a result of that loss. If Bill Clinton had followed even a basic legislative strategy, he would have secured passage of some kind of comprehensive healthcare plan. If he had only negotiated and compromised with Jim McDermott and the other 90 co-sponsors of the alternate bill, surely they could have all agreed on some acceptable amendments.

I am convinced beyond a shadow of a doubt that if Bill Clinton had scored a major victory early in his first term (especially with his self-proclaimed legislative healthcare centerpiece), he would have become pumped up with a sense of victory and possibility and fired up enough to have immediately grabbed another major issue by the horns. I believe that Bill Clinton would have loaded his legislative tray like a college football player grabs food in the cafeteria line.

I BELIEVE THAT BILL CLINTON WOULD HAVE LOADED HIS LEGISLATIVE TRAY LIKE A COLLEGE FOOTBALL PLAYER GRABS FOOD IN THE CAFETERIA LINE.

Lyndon Johnson complained that every issue on his presidential desk was already an issue before he began his career 26 years earlier. He grabbed a big tray and loaded up dozens of America's accumulated problems and proceeded to deal with them one by one in quick succession. He had tasted victory, and he was on a roll.

Johnson was so successful that one of the dissertations I reviewed for this book explored essentially one question:

Was the 98th Congress properly acting as a counterbalance to the president? Johnson was so successful that some people were concerned that Congress had ceased to function at all, and that it was merely a rubber stamp for President Johnson. Dr. Borst's conclusion was that Congress was still performing its role, but to a large extent, Johnson was performing his role so well that it gave the appearance of congressional malfunction. That is how well Lyndon Johnson led.

---

*There's nothing like a couple of wins to put a spring in your step.*

— CHARLES KRAUTHAMMER

---

Given that there was a much larger pile of accumulated and unresolved issues in 1992 and given that Bill Clinton had so much more charismatic horsepower than Lyndon Johnson, I believe that if he were flush with a major success under his belt, Bill Clinton could have run the legislative table for eight years and passed more significant legislation than even President Johnson. That did not happen, and that is what I feel was the greatest failure of the Clinton administration, and ultimately America's biggest loss.

Presidents like Franklin Roosevelt and Lyndon Johnson only come around once in a while. When that happens, the country needs to reap the benefits of having those special leaders. Bill Clinton (I believe) was meant to be one of those leaders, and I am sure that he would have been if he had scored an early victory and developed momentum.

However, healthcare failed, and it failed spectacularly. Clinton never again attempted to tackle a major piece of legislation. Like every other president, he did pass some bills such as NAFTA and the Family Medical Leave Act. However, the big ones like energy, funding for social security, or even another attempt at comprehensive healthcare, etc. would be left for future presidents.

I am convinced that Bill Clinton was not emotionally prepared to experience another major rejection and setback. The healthcare loss set the tone for the rest of his presidency. If he had been properly prepared and had developed a sensible legislative strategy for healthcare, I believe that the "state of our union" today would be significantly different and better. If you measure what **could** (and should) have happened against what actually did happen during the Clinton years, it is easy to feel frustrated and short changed.

Avoiding additional "missed opportunities" like the ones that we experienced in the Carter and Clinton administrations is the goal of this book. If a future president follows the ten point legislative checklist, he or she will probably have a very good chance of successfully passing legislation. When success comes early, it can create its own momentum for passing additional bills — if the president capitalizes quickly.

## CONCLUSION

Being President of the United States is probably the most difficult, complex, and challenging job in the world. Any job requires a certain set of skills in order to perform the necessary tasks. If a president is not properly prepared to seek congressional passage of the agenda that he or she campaigned for, then there is an excellent chance that America will experience more missed opportunities — opportunities that we can no longer afford to miss!

---

### An American Citizen's Request To Our President

Please pay attention to what has worked well in the past. Look into the future and tell us what you see; tell us what we should do and why we should do it; learn the rules of engagement in Washington; use common sense; show respect; let the process be open; keep it simple; don't forget what time it is; other people also have good ideas — listen to them; compromise and negotiation are tools, not enemies; and don't forget that America wants to be a good neighbor!

— Bill Porter, An American Citizen

---

*All great change in America begins
at the dinner table.*

— RONALD REAGAN

*The genius of the United States is not best or most in its executives
or legislatures, nor in its ambassadors or authors or colleges, or
churches, or parlors, nor even in its newspapers or inventors, but
always most in the common people.*

— WALT WHITMAN

## CHAPTER SEVEN

# A NEW IDEA
# FOR AMERICA

*Sometimes if you want to see a change for the better,
you have to take things into your own hands.*

— CLINT EASTWOOD

*"Ideas won't keep; something must be done about them."*

— ALFRED NORTH WHITEHEAD,
ENGLISH PHILOSOPHER AND MATHEMATICIAN (1861 - 1947)

## A NEW IDEA FOR AMERICA

We have all said at one time, "Hey, I have an idea!" Too often, however, we do not take action, and it is soon forgotten. Well, I have an idea that I believe can significantly improve our role as citizens, significantly improve the quality of our presidential candidates, and significantly improve their chances of successfully gaining passage of their campaign agendas. If you agree, we should take action.

## THE PLAN

Step one of the ten point check list for developing a presidential legislative strategy is to successfully sell the idea to the voters during the campaign. This lays the foundation that the other nine steps will build upon. That has not been happening for the past several elections, and it is one of the main reasons that so many of our national problems remain unresolved.

Unfortunately, today's candidates have all learned a

> *Never say anything in a national campaign*
> *that anyone might remember.*
>
> — Eugene J. McCarthy (Democratic Candidate for President, 1968)

basic fact; if they take a clear position on **any issue**, they will lose some voters in the general election. For example, if a candidate states that he or she is in favor of (or against) abortion, there are some voters who will not care what else the candidate may stand for, and they will vote for or against that candidate strictly on their position on that one issue. Gun control, gay marriage, national healthcare, immigration and taxation are other good examples of issues that will cause some voters to vote against a presidential candidate.

The candidates are not stupid. They now know to talk only in generalities and, at all costs, avoid any specific recommendations. Their goal, or election strategy, is to get to November without losing any voters because they were foolish enough to lay out their positions and real intentions.

This is not an attempt to single out Senator Obama, because all of the candidates are equally guilty, but his campaign slogan, "Change We Can Believe In" dramatically makes the point. What change? Is that a new program or a new federal agency? What will he do specifically that will be a change? Shouldn't we get to know that sort of thing before we vote? Senator McCain's "Straight Talk Express" slogan sounds good just like "Change We Can Believe In" sounds good. But what do we know now that we did not know before we heard them?

Most people would agree that we should know (and so should the candidates themselves) what they really intend to do as president. There is a very simple idea that can make all of that happen.

The big facilitator of this campaign tool will be the media who most Americans agree are currently performing substantially below their potential. Television, talk radio, newspapers, magazines, periodicals and newsletters could provide the vehicle that would ratchet up the election process several notches.

It is important to recognize that the election process itself can be a critical factor in the eventual success or failure of a presidential administration. For example, if Americans were convinced during a campaign that we should challenge the Russians in space or that we were going to make many substantial and specific changes in our conservation, production, and expansion of the variety of our sources of energy, then the president would have been already on the way to making it happen — not home free, but definitely on the way!

The current dynamics of presidential campaigns rob the candidates of that opportunity and rob us of the benefits that could have accrued. Instead of vague generalities, murky messages, and verbal magic, we deserve and need specifics. Here is what we can do.

*The reduction of political discourse to sound bites is one of the worst things that's happened in American political life.*

— John Silber

## Countdown To The Presidency

There could be a ten week period in August, September, and October when only one of the top ten issues will be discussed or at least be the featured issue of the week. Each of the candidates will know that every interview on television that week will be focused on that specific issue. There will be nowhere to hide. We, and the candidates themselves, will get a clear chance to see if they understand the issue, have a real plan, and if the plan is better or the same as the other candidate's plan.

This would be a great opportunity for the media to prepare informative shows or articles that give us, the voters, a real chance to understand the background and future implications of certain problems or issues. For example, just what are the real facts about out current immigration policies (both legal and illegal)? What are the real costs of illegal immigrants (all costs)? What are the real benefits? Is legal immigration addressing our worker needs with a plan (i.e. engineers, scientists, etc.)? Are we targeting for specific worker skills that are in short supply, or is it just luck of the draw?

If Americans knew more about the issues, then we could make better decisions. Candidates would know that we will want to hear exactly what they will do about an issue if they are elected. That means that they will actually have to have a real plan — not just some glib, prepackaged sound-bite that sounds good but says nothing.

For example, at the end of each week, the major television networks (both cable and traditional) could have a show that might give each candidate a half hour or hour each — without interruptions — to speak to the American people about that one particular issue. The candidates would have to significantly improve their game, or they would be exposed as unprepared or incompetent. They would need to be able to discuss the issue for at least thirty minutes or more. That means they would really have to be knowledgeable. The additional preparation that they would need would force them to improve their own thinking on each of the major issues.

Who would decide on the top ten issues? Perhaps five television networks could participate, and they each could pick two. Perhaps the candidates could each pick five. That would give us some insight into their personal agendas. Maybe there could be a website where citizens could choose. Maybe the Democrats and Republicans could each pick five. It doesn't really matter as long as ten major issues get a thorough treatment by the media and the candidates.

## Media Opportunity

It would also give members of the media a chance to display their capabilities and professionalism. How informative and unbiased were their reports on each of the issues? How skillful and insightful were their interviewers and reporters? Like with sports, Americans could be discussing the great or poor job that a network or candidate did the night before as well as the issue itself. Those focused weekly discussions would be a great improvement. Unlike sport shows which only provide entertainment, these shows could be entertaining and also help the country significantly improve its chances of a better future.

## The Presidential Olympics

The media should be all over this idea like green on grass because it would be novel, and people would tune in just to see what it is all about. This would be a major boost for their advertising income. It would be up to each of the members of the media to do a good job, so their audience would tune in the following week.

Like the Olympics, this event would only happen every four years, so it would give the media an excellent chance to prepare for each presidential election. In depth and interesting background stories could be invaluable as campaign tools.

For example, what are the major advantages and disadvantages of wind, solar, hydrogen, geothermal, nuclear, coal, wave, oil, hydroelectric, and other sources of energy? What would it cost to set up the infrastructure to have filling stations all over the country that could refuel a hydrogen powered automobile? Is it feasible? We don't know because no one is informing us. We need to do better!

The major advantage of a ten week countdown of top ten issues is that it offers a maximum opportunity for the candidates to build a solid foundation with the voters. Both candidates will have to go through this process, so they will have no choice but to lay out their plans for each issue. The process — not the candidates — will dictate the way the campaign is conducted.

In an age of instant polls, it will be easy to know that the president-elect will have connected with the American public on some issues more than with others. This will help the new president to know which policies to pursue first. It would probably make sense to start with the ones that received the most public support. Pass the easy ones first, and thus generate momentum. If Bill Clinton had this tool, it could have been a different ball game.

This is America. We are not limited to whatever the media and the politicians throw at us. We are not stuck in their paradigm. I am convinced that there is indeed change that we can believe in and that straight talk is good. However, I want to know what it is and whether or not a particular candidate is likely to make it happen — before I vote for them. This plan could be a step in the right direction. There may be better plans. If so, let's talk! Quickly!

■  ■  ■

*I have an old-fashioned belief that Americans like to make up their own minds on the basis of all available information. The conclusions you draw are your own affair. I have no desire to influence them, and shall leave such efforts to those who have more confidence in their own judgment than I have in mine.*

— Edward R. Murrow

*The stationary condition is the beginning of the end.*
— HENRI AMIEL

*Change is not made without inconvenience, even from worse to better.*
— RICHARD HOOKER

# THOUGHTS ABOUT CHANGE

*Drastic action may be costly, but it can be less expensive than continuing inaction.*
— RICHARD E. NEUSTADT

*Men are not prisoners of fate, but only prisoners of their own mind.*
— FRANKLIN DELANO ROOSEVELT

*The future must be shaped or it will impose itself as catastrophe.*
— HENRY A. KISSINGER

*The people who are crazy enough to think they can change the world are the ones who do.*
— APPLE COMPUTER, INC.

*It is a secret, both in nature and state, that it is safer to change many things than one.*
— FRANCIS BACON

*All our hopes for the future depend on a sound understanding of the past.*
— FREDERIC HARRISON

■ ■ ■

*The laws of nature and the universe*
*apply to animals, people*
*and nations ...*

Every morning in Africa,
a gazelle wakes up.
It knows that it must run
faster than the fastest lion
or it will be killed.

Every morning in Africa,
a lion wakes up.
It knows it must outrun
the slowest gazelle or
it will starve to death.

It doesn't matter whether
you are a lion or a gazelle.
When the sun comes up,
you better start running.

— UNKNOWN

*As other countries around the world*
*pick up speed, America has no choice but to*
*set new goals, dig deeper, strive harder,*
*and achieve new standards of excellence.*

■  ■  ■

# BOOK SERIES DESCRIPTION & PREVIEWS

## AMERICA — A TRILOGY

### The past, present and future!

*Presidential Lessons Learned - Follow The Leader* assesses the leadership strengths and weaknesses of four former Presidents.

The second book will take stock of our current national opportunities and offer ten new ideas.

The third book will help us determine our future role as an international neighbor.

■ ■ ■

*Great change dominates the world, and unless we move with change we will become its victims.*

— ROBERT F. KENNEDY

BOOK #2

# HELLO AMERICA ... TODAY IS YESTERDAY'S TOMORROW!

"Yesterday" as a country, we have repeatedly said, in effect, we would deal with our problems "tomorrow." Well, today is yesterday's tomorrow! Problems have been put off and delayed for too many years. The time for procrastination is over. Let's not wait for the future to happen to us; let's go and create it!

Our next book will discuss ten new ideas that can significantly improve America. Most of the ideas are interrelated, and all of them will require a major change or adjustment in our traditional thinking. Collectively, they can save our country over a trillion dollars a year. Unless one believes that all of America's problems can be solved with just a little tinkering here and there, then real change will be required.

## CHANGE

*A challenge to the adventurous,*
*An opportunity to the alert,*
*And a threat to the insecure.*

— ANONYMOUS

*Where there is no vision, the people perish ...*

— BIBLE PROVERBS 29:18

## THE TEN "TRILLION DOLLAR" IDEAS FOR AMERICA

1. An interconnected interstate water system.

2. A ten-year strategy for energy independence.

3. Fifty new cities (one per state). Why?

4. Immigration — an international talent raid.

5. The professionalization of education.

6. A new post-cold war foreign policy.

7. Factories in prisons.

8. Establishment of a wealth creation index.

9. A practical approach to healthcare.

10. A way to save American jobs, eliminate the trade deficit, and help fund Social Security — using the same tool.

> ## *BONUS IDEA
> A simple, more productive, less expensive
> and more equitable tax system.

*There's a way to do it better ... find it.*

— THOMAS A. EDISON

*The world basically and fundamentally is constituted on the basis of harmony.  Everything works in co-operation with something else.*

— PRESTON BRADLEY

## BOOK #3

# HELLO INTERNATIONAL NEIGHBORS ... DO YOU SEE WHAT WE SEE?

Having lived in Europe for nearly 12 years, my family and I learned firsthand that the European view of America is significantly different than the perception we have of ourselves.  Being immersed for a dozen years in the cultures of many other countries provided us an opportunity to re-examine Americanized assumptions that we would have normally never thought to challenge or question.

Living abroad and vacationing abroad are two distinct events.  Interacting on a day to day basis with the citizens of different countries, reading their newspapers, and watching their television shows (especially the news), provided us with a rare opportunity to look at America through the eyes of our international neighbors.  We were able to objectively assess America as well as other countries, their citizens, and their cultures.

For example, in 1990, our family had not yet embraced the idea of recycling.  We were clearly out of place (and outside of the law) in Europe.  We soon adapted and quickly became true believers.  Visiting friends and family in America, who had still not made the transition, now caused us to view the "American way" as not always the best way.

On the other hand, we also noticed that most Americans work harder and longer than many of our European counterparts. There were many other observations that caused us to pause. Many times, "the American way" seemed to be the best choice. However, there were other instances when it became clear to us that sometimes other cultures have discovered a better or more effective way. Our experience made us keenly aware that everyone has something to offer and that no one is always right.

During our sojourn, our son attended European schools for eight years and also spent four years at an American High School on a U.S. Army base. His bilingual and bicultural experience exposed huge differences in expectations, discipline, and achievement between the school systems. It became obvious that America needs to upgrade its educational system quickly, or our children will be unable to compete in the future as adults.

The entire 12 year experience pointed out both the need and the advantages for America to have a deeper dialogue and cultural exchange with the rest of the world. It is clear to me that most Americans do not have an accurate perception of the people and cultures in other parts of the world and that those countries also have a distorted view of the United States.

The media in all countries have their own biases and agendas. The "news" that is reported about a world event is, many times, portrayed differently in various countries.

Too often, the "news" depends on how the members of the media want their viewers or readers to react. Creating or manipulating the news in order to generate a desired public opinion is prevalent in all countries. Unfortunately, the media's selective reporting and deliberate distortions leave the citizens in all countries with a less than accurate understanding of themselves, their neighbors and the world at large. The media will always be imperfect because of the human factor. However, there is both the need and the opportunity to continually improve the interaction and understanding between members of the world community. That is the purpose of our third book in this series.

At this complex point in world history, most people would agree that more dialogue and less suspicion would help to improve the future of mankind. In order to promote more conversation and interaction, as well as more awareness and cooperation, our third book in this series will compile the interviews of 25 of the world's most important leaders (both government and civilian). The interviews will focus on their views of America, their perceptions of their own countries as members of the world community, and what they think both countries should do to improve the future for their citizens.

The questions and discussion points will be the same for each leader. This will provide us with the opportunity to analyze the responses and compile a composite of how the world sees America, how other countries see themselves, and how they feel that the international neighborhood can be improved.

■　■　■

# NOTES

*Success is the sum of detail.*

— HARVEY S. FIRESTONE

■   ■   ■

# NOTES

## PREFACE

    1.  US Bureau of Labor Statistics.

## CHAPTER ONE

1. James MacGregor Burns, seminal work on leadership. <u>Leadership.</u> Harper and Row, 1978.
2. James MacGregor Burns, <u>Transforming Leadership</u> (p.23) Grove Press, 2003.
3. Ibid.
4. Burns, J.M. and Sorenson, G.J., <u>Dead Center: Clinton/Gore leadership and the perils of moderation.</u> A Lisa Drew Book/Scribner, 1999.
5. James MacGregor Burns, <u>Running Alone</u>. Basic Books, of the Perseus Book Group, 2006.
6. U.S. News and World Report, June 26, 2006, (p. 72).
7. James MacGregor Burns, <u>Running Alone</u>. Basic Books, of the Perseus Book Group, 2006.

## CONGRESSIONAL TIME LINE

Sources for the Presidential Time Line, <u>World Almanac</u>, 2008 and Carter Smith, <u>Presidents, All You Need to Know</u>, 2005.

## CHAPTER TWO

1. Young, Silcock, and Dunn, Journey to Tranquility, (p. 68).
2. John Logsdon, <u>The Apollo Decision and its Lessons for Policy-Makers.</u> The George Washington University – NASA Grant No. 09-010-030, (p. 12) 1970.
3. Carter Smith, <u>Presidents,</u> Hylas Publishing, 2005, (p. 212).
4. Ibid.

5. John Logston, <u>The Decision to Go to the Moon</u>.
   The MIT Press, 1970 (p. 65).
6. Ibid. (p. 67).
7. New York Times, September 21, 1960.
8. John Kennedy, Inaugural Address, Jan. 20, 1961.
9. Ibid.
10. Richard Scott Harris, <u>Lawrence F. O'Brien, the Democratic Party and the Nation</u>. Dissertation, University of Texas at Austin, 1998, (p. 184).
11. Ibid.
12. Ibid.
13. Time Magazine, February 17, 1961.
14. Lawrence O'Brien, <u>No Final Victories</u>. 1974, (p. 99).
15. John Logsdon, <u>The Apollo Decision and its Lessons for Policy-Makers</u>. The George Washington University – NASA Grant No. 09-010-030, (p. 6) 1970.
16. Time Magazine, July 2, 2007 (p. 50).
17. U.S. Congress, Senate Committee on Aeronautical and Space Sciences, Documents on the International Aspects of the Exploration and Use of Outer Space, 1954-1962, 88th Congress, 1st session, 1963, Doc.18, (p. 329).

## CHAPTER THREE

1. Tip O'Neill, <u>Man of the House</u>. Random House, 1987, (p. 179).
2. James MacGregor Burns, <u>Running Alone</u>. Basic Books, of the Perseus Book Group, 2006, (p. 78).
3. Lyndon Johnson, Address before a joint session of Congress, November 27, 1963.
4. Ibid.
5. Ibid.
6. Brinkley, A. & Davis, D. <u>The American Presidency.</u> Houghton Mifflin Company, 2004, (p. 412).
7. Lyndon Johnson, Inaugural address, January 20, 1965.
8. Brinkley, A. & Davis, D. <u>The American Presidency.</u> Houghton Mifflin Company, 2004, (p. 417).
9. James MacGregor Burns, <u>Running Alone</u>. Basic Books, of the Perseus Book Group, 2006, (p. 83).

10. Joseph A. Califano, Jr., <u>Inside: A Public and Private Life</u>. Public Affairs 2004, (p. 155).

11. Ibid. (p. 153).

12. Richard Scott Harris, <u>Lawrence F. O'Brien, the Democratic Party and the Nation.</u> Dissertation, University of Texas at Austin, 1998, (p. 318).

13. Tip O'Neill, <u>Man of the House</u>. Random House, 1987, (p. 187).

14. Richard Scott Harris, <u>Lawrence F. O'Brien, the Democratic Party and the Nation</u>. Dissertation, University of Texas at Austin, 1998, (p. 335).

15. Eric Lyle Davis, <u>Building Presidential Coalitions in Congress: Legislative Liaison in the Johnson White House</u>. Dissertation, 1977, (p. 113).

16. Ibid. (p.165).

17. Joseph A. Califano, Jr., <u>Inside: A Public and Private Life</u>. Public Affairs 2004, (p. 186).

18. Brinkley, A. & Davis, D. <u>The American Presidency</u>. Houghton Mifflin Company, 2004, (p. 415).

19. Tip O'Neill, <u>Man of the House</u>. Random House, 1987, (p. 185).

## CHAPTER FOUR

1. John Costley Barrow, III, <u>An Era of Limits: Jimmy Carter and the Quest for a National Energy Policy</u>. Dissertation, 1996, (p. 9).

2. Ibid. (p. 11).

3. Ibid. (p. 12).

4. Nixon: More Money, More Action for "Clean Energy," Congressional Quarterly, June 11, 1971, (pp. 1284 – 88).

5. John Costley Barrow, III, <u>An Era of Limits: Jimmy Carter and the Quest for a National Energy Policy</u>. Dissertation, 1996, (p. 22).

6. Ibid. (p. 25).

7. Ibid. (p. 29).

8. Ibid. (p. 34).

9. Public Papers of the Presidents of the United States, Gerald R. Ford 1976 – 1977, (p. 448).

10. John Costley Barrow, III, <u>An Era of Limits: Jimmy Carter and the Quest for a National Energy Policy</u>. Dissertation, 1996, (p. 39).

11. Ibid. (p. 50).

12. New York Times, December 24, 1976, (p. A11).

13. Ibid. (p. A18).

14. John Costley Barrow, III, <u>An Era of Limits: Jimmy Carter and the Quest for a National Energy Policy</u>. Dissertation, 1996, (p. 57).

15. New York Times, January 27, 1977, (p. 1).

16. James MacGregor Burns, <u>Running Alone</u>. Basic Books, of the Perseus Book Group, 2006, (p. 124).

17. Joseph A. Califano, Jr., <u>Inside: A Public and Private Life</u>. Public Affairs 2004, (p. 334).

18. Tip O'Neill, <u>Man of the House</u>. Random House, 1987, (p. 297).

19. Ibid. (p. 302).

20. Brinkley, A. & Davis, D. <u>The American Presidency.</u> Houghton Mifflin Company, 2004, (p. 459).

21. Congressional Quarterly, February 26, 1977, (p. 362).

22. Joseph A. Califano, Jr., <u>Inside: A Public and Private Life</u>. Public Affairs 2004, (p. 332).

23. Tip O'Neill, <u>Man of the House</u>. Random House, 1987, (p. 308).

24. Ibid. (p. 311).

25. Ibid.

26. John Costley Barrow, III, <u>An Era of Limits: Jimmy Carter and the Quest for a National Energy Policy</u>. Dissertation, 1996, (p. 77).

27. Ibid. (p. 81).

28. New York Times, January 27, 1977, (p. 1).

29. John Costley Barrow, III, <u>An Era of Limits: Jimmy Carter and the Quest for a National Energy Policy</u>. Dissertation, 1996, (p. 111).

30. Congressional Quarterly Weekly, October 8, 1977, (p. 2121).

31. Tip O'Neill, <u>Man of the House</u>. Random House, 1987, (p. 330).

32. Jimmy Carter, <u>Keeping Faith: Memoirs of a President</u>. Bantam Books, 1982, (p. 111).

33. John Costley Barrow, III, <u>An Era of Limits: Jimmy Carter and the Quest for a National Energy Policy</u>. Dissertation, 1996, (p. 182).
34. Public Papers of the Presidents, Jimmy Carter, 1979, (pp.1235 – 41).
35. Atlanta Journal Constitution, February 25, 2007, (p. F4).
36.  Ibid.  January 7, 2007, (p. C7).

## CHAPTER FIVE

1. <u>Time Magazine</u>, October, 2007.
2. <u>"U.S. Health Care Spending in an International Context,"</u> Health Affairs, vol. 23 (2004) (pp. 10-25).
3. Atlanta Journal Constitution, March 16, 2006, (p. 1).
4. Kimberly Weathers, <u>Fitting an Elephant through a Keyhole: America's Struggle with National Health Insurance in the Twentieth Century</u>.  Dissertation, 2004, (p. 150).
5. Ibid. (p. 161).
6. Richard Nixon, Message to Congress, February 6, 1974.
7. New York Times, February 4, 1974, (p. L 29).
8. Kimberly Weathers, <u>Fitting an Elephant through a Keyhole: America's Struggle with National Health Insurance in the Twentieth Century</u>.  Dissertation, 2004, (p. 223).
9. Ibid. (p. 223).
10. Burns, J.M. and Sorenson, G.J., <u>Dead Center: Clinton/Gore leadership and the perils of moderation</u>.  A Lisa Drew Book/ Scribner, 1999, (p. 131).
11. Public Opinion Quarterly, 1999, vol. 63, (p. 237).
12. Kimberly Weathers, <u>Fitting an Elephant through a Keyhole: America's Struggle with National Health Insurance in the Twentieth Century</u>.  Dissertation, 2004, (p. 263).
13. Burns, J.M. and Sorenson, G.J., <u>Dead Center: Clinton/Gore leadership and the perils of moderation</u>.  A Lisa Drew Book/ Scribner, 1999, (p. 130).
14. Ibid.
15. Kimberly Weathers, <u>Fitting an Elephant through a Keyhole: America's Struggle with National Health Insurance in the Twentieth Century</u>.  Dissertation, 2004, (p. 274).

16. Burns, J.M. and Sorenson, G.J., <u>Dead Center: Clinton/Gore leadership and the perils of moderation</u>. A Lisa Drew Book/Scribner, 1999, (p. 126).

17. Kimberly Weathers, <u>Fitting an Elephant through a Keyhole: America's Struggle with National Health Insurance in the Twentieth Century</u>. Dissertation, 2004, (p. 276).

18. Ibid. (p. 292).

19. Ibid.

## CHAPTER SIX

1. Donald Riddle, The Presidency of Lyndon B. Johnson. American Government Annual, 1965-66, (p. 64).

2. Brinkley, A. & Davis, D. <u>The American Presidency</u>. Houghton Mifflin Company, 2004, (p. 417).

■  ■  ■